ADVENTURES OF A DRAG QUEEN

Jeff Kristian

A MR BINKS MEDIA BOOK

Copyright © Mr Binks Media 2019
Cover design © Mr Binks Media 2019

First Edition
Edited by Robert Ingham

All rights reserved. No part of this publication may be reproduced, stored in a retrieval system, or transmitted in any form or by any means, electronic, mechanical, photocopy, recording or otherwise, without prior written permission of the copyright owner. Nor can it be circulated in any form of binding or cover other than that in which it is published and without similar condition including this condition being imposed on a subsequent purchaser.

British Library Cataloguing in Publication Data.
A catalogue record for this book is available from the British Library.

ISBN 978-0-9928456-5-0 (Paperback Edition)
ISBN 978-0-9928456-6-7 (eBook Edition)

Mr Binks Media
mrbinksmedia@jeffkristian.com

I DEDICATE THIS BOOK TO ALL BUDDING NEW DRAG QUEENS

"Brace yourselves… it's an awfully big adventure!"

www.jeffkristian.com

AUTHOR'S PROLOGUE

It wasn't easy for me to begin working in drag. Aside from writing songs, I'd already been performing as an actor and singer for many years, but the transition to high heels and a dress left a not-so glamorous taste in my mouth. I can liken it to my formative years at school, kissing a girlfriend; outwardly doing something acceptable while inwardly knowing it wasn't really where my tongue should be. Indeed, when dragging up to pay the rent looked to be my only option, many people around me expressed the opinion that as a gay man, I surely should be gagging to dress as a woman. They seemed almost disappointed when I revealed this wasn't the case. It was only when a fellow actor suggested I distinguish the difference between profession and vocation that everything fell into place. They were not frocks but costumes, like a pantomime dame. The outrage of professional drag was to dress like a woman but act like a man. Over a quarter of a century later, this early turmoil seems almost laughable when measured against the bigger picture.

A few years ago, I ended a fifteen-year residency at Soho's flagship cabaret haunt Molly Moggs Theatre Bar, smack bang in the middle of central London's glittering nightlife. With my creative juices already squirting in many other directions, it seemed as good a time as any to hang up my stilettos for the final time. I'd secretly been looking forward to doing this for quite a while but, in so doing, it brought to the surface several emotions that I wasn't expecting. It forced me to reflect not only on my own career but British drag in its entirety.

Drag has been good to me, but it has also brought problems. Any performer will understand typecasting, and this has been a biggie for me. It kept me working which is a blessing, as any actor will tell you, but it has overshadowed much of my non-drag work and made it difficult for people to perceive me in any other way. For a while, even my agent only sent me cross-dressing roles. It's not easy to spread your wings as an actor when they're weighed down with heavy sequins.

That said I'm very proud of my work as a female impersonator, although I feel I've taken it as far as it can go. A decade of stand-up comedy in cabaret and theatre; appearances in film playing drag, transgender and female roles; three telly seasons as Big Brother's Singing Drag Queen on 'Bit On The Side'. I grabbed my crotch as Madonna in a golden corset on a trestle table in front of five Mayors of London. I made a little disco dolly faint into the orchestra pit when I appeared on stage as Cher for the launch of her Greatest Hits DVD. I opened a supermarket, I appeared in a couple of television commercials… I even won an award. And for five years, I wrote a regular column about my drag adventures for an online LGBT+ magazine, many of which are featured in this book. But having plunged into drag after ten years singing with bands, I arrived as an outsider and remained that way pretty much until the end. This has perhaps given me an opportunity to observe from the wings in a way that is not possible for everyone. What I've seen made my decision to finally lose the beehive a little easier.

There is a kind of public complacency towards drag queens in the UK. Over time, I've come to realise that it hangs on the uniquely British pub culture. Whatever way you look at it, the condescending mind-set that drag queens are nothing more than a cheap pub turn will probably never go away. I'm not talking about seasoned actors like Michael Ball taking on the traditional drag role of Edna Turnblad in 'Hairspray', or indeed David Suchet turning 'The Importance of Being Earnest' on its perfectly coiffured head in the role of Lady Bracknell. It's relatively easy to dip a fishnet-clad toe in the drag river for a short season. I'm talking about the grass roots of drag, working queens making their on-going living in cabaret up and down the country; Britain's drag backbone, if you like. And I'm not the only one to have noticed this. Back in the nineties, I publicly countersigned a petition by Paul O'Grady referring to his role as Lily Savage, the gist of which bemoaned how drag queens were being taken for granted by members of their own community. Suggesting how we would spend all year entertaining, performing, raising money and awareness for charity, always on call without question for little or no money every day of the year, including Christmas and New Year, and yet still be hustled like cattle. It was a call to boycott London Pride, which we did… for a while. Pride without drag queens? People have been medicated for less.

Upon reflection, despite being a cry to be taken seriously as professional artists, I think O'Grady's event in the national press strangely contributed towards the blurring of edges between seasoned professional drag actors and our nation's gloriously dressed party goers. Nowadays it would seem every bloke in a bra is a drag queen, regardless of any kind of structured act, performance or role. Though perhaps it's a good thing that people are increasingly able to do this. With the much-needed rise of drag culture in British living rooms through television, most recently with shows such as 'Ru Paul's Drag Race', comes a lowering of resistance towards the LGBTQ community (the Q by the way, stands for Questioning, not Queer). Even if we're all tarred with the same hanky-flapping brush, the more we are seen the better we can integrate. My role on 'Bit On The Side' had a mixed international reaction; everything from requests for extravagant sex to death threats. A man in Charleston, South Carolina publicly suggested he'd like to string me up by the neck from a tree and shoot me in the face... social media at its most gracious! Needless to say, I didn't tell him where I lived. Ironically the following year, Gsus Lopez's film 'Out', in which I played distraught single-mother Mary, won the Best Fashion Film award at Charleston Fashion Week. A stiletto-clad step in the right direction, I guess?

Boy George was once quoted as saying that drag queens make a bigger political statement than any politician. If that's true, then perhaps my tiny contribution has made a difference to people's lives in a way I could never have foreseen. My show has had its last curtain call for now, but thankfully our legacy continues. So the next time a gentleman in a frock gives his all to entertain you, please be kind and remember: you're riding the back of a much bigger global undercurrent, good manners and a little respect are required. After all... drag queens are for life, not just for Christmas.

All that said, here I am more than twenty-five years after those first doubts, with damaged feet from thousands of performances in unnaturally high shoes, a lack of natural eyelashes following years of gluing on falsies, constant back pain and chest hair that will strangely not grow back properly, but I guess I'm still proud to have been a part of the whole extraordinary shebang. As much as I hate to admit it, it has enriched my life and changed me as a person. It's toughened me up a great deal. And it's disciplined me in respect to my attitude and demeanour. But perhaps most endearingly, it's made me not take myself quite so seriously as I used to. It's also made me see and reflect upon life in a slightly off-centre way. I now view our little planet and the people who inhabit it through drag-tinted spectacles, as it were. And as I advance in years, I kind of like it!

So welcome to my un-hinged little world. Here are some of my adventures, my anecdotes, my opinions and my observations; a little exaggerated, a bit extreme and in no particular order. I hope you enjoy reading them as much as I have enjoyed living them.

MRS CRABTREE'S PEACH TREE

I diligently weighed up the odds with a cabbage in one hand and a cauliflower in the other. I just couldn't for the life of me remember which of the two my dinner guest had said she couldn't eat. An allergy to one of them apparently makes her fall to the floor grasping her throat and gasping for air. The thought did cross my mind to buy both just so as to have something entertaining on standby in case conversation got boring. But I'd already been in Tesco Express for half an hour trying to decide. And the look on the face of Kevin, the youth wearing the Fruit and Veg Technical Supervisor badge, clearly demonstrated I had already contravened the "express" part of my understanding with this particular branch of Tesco. He wrinkled his nose at me from behind a stack of budget toilet rolls on the end of aisle seven as I pondered how he might technically supervise a carrot or an apple.

I suddenly became aware of movement in my shopping basket. I looked down to see a big green woolen bobble atop a matching knitted hat. At first, I thought it was a child having a rummage through my shopping. But instead, a petite wrinkled elderly woman glanced cheekily up at me, holding one of my peaches aloft before plunging her two or three remaining front teeth into it. It was a bit of a shock, like being accosted by a naughty little pixie.

'I don't mind you having a peach love, but I haven't paid for it yet,' I said. She chuckled and turned, took aim and threw the remains of the peach across the aisle. A broad woman in dungarees spun around as it hit her squarely on the back of the head.

'I'm not having all this again, Mrs Crabtree,' she cursed in a raised voice. 'Come here.' The woman stepped forward to take hold of Mrs Crabtree, but she was having none of it. She grabbed onto my basket and swung back, promptly landing in a big tray of mushrooms, pulling both me and my basket with her. My tin of mushy peas dropped to the floor and rolled up the aisle, bringing additional stress to an already vexed Kevin.

'She's always showing me up like this in public. Sorry mate,' said the woman.

'Don't worry,' I replied, 'I was more concerned that I'd hurt her.'

'Oh don't worry about her, she's got Alzheimer's. She'll have forgot about it in an hour. Get up you stupid woman!' She hauled Mrs Crabtree from the mushroom tray. 'You wouldn't believe she used to be an Ambulance driver in the war, would you?' I thought for a moment of our gracious monarch Queen Elizabeth and her wartime driving adventures, clearly a little more respected.

'Are you her daughter?' I asked.

'Oh God, no. She didn't have kids. She said children would cramp her style. Cause too much grief and trouble.' I thought of our poor gracious monarch again. 'Though she's been married four times in four different continents. Don't look like she'd have it in her, does she?'

At this moment Kevin approached with another man in a black suit and tie. 'Excuse me Sir,' he said. 'I'm afraid that if you can't respect our mushrooms I'm going to have to remove your basket and ask you to vacate our premises.'

'It wasn't me, it was Mrs Crabtree here,' I said, pointing.

'Oh that's it, blame this poor senile old lady,' said the dungaree-clad woman, blushing slightly. The man in the suit nodded in agreement. I looked at Mrs Crabtree. She looked back up at me innocently, as though butter wouldn't melt in her slightly gurning mouth. As her head gently wobbled, her bright green bobble swung about aimlessly on the last little thread keeping it attached. Her eyes blinked several times, waiting for my response.

'Yes, I'm sorry' I said, 'I lost my balance for a moment. I'll pay for any damage.' Mrs Crabtree smiled. She waddled back to the fruit section and took a moment to select me a replacement peach which she then gently placed in my basket, her crystal blue eyes sparkling up at me.

'Come on,' said the woman. Grabbing her by the arm, she whisked Mrs Crabtree up the aisle and away.

But then a curious thing happened. Just before she disappeared from view, Mrs Crabtree smiled back at me and winked. A very knowledgeable, worldly-wise wink.

Looking back, I don't believe this shrunken old lady was senile. I think she was an adventurer, making the most of the few remaining moments of adventure she had left. I planted the pip from the tiny Mrs Crabtree's peach. And after a few weeks, I had a tiny tree. Mrs Crabtree's Peach Tree. I thought of her every time I watered it. And I'm grateful she selected me to play a part in the adventure that was her life.

At this moment Kevin approached with another man in a black suit and tie. 'Excuse me Sir,' he said. 'I'm afraid that if you can't respect our mushrooms I'm going to have to remove your basket and ask you to vacate our premises.'

'It wasn't me, it was Mrs Crabtree here,' I said, pointing.

'Oh that's it, blame this poor senile old lady,' said the dungaree-clad woman, blushing slightly. The man in the suit nodded in agreement. I looked at Mrs Crabtree. She looked back up at me innocently, as though butter wouldn't melt in her slightly gurning mouth. As her head gently wobbled, her bright green bobble swung about aimlessly on the last little thread keeping it attached. Her eyes blinked several times, waiting for my response.

'Yes, I'm sorry' I said, 'I lost my balance for a moment. I'll pay for any damage.' Mrs Crabtree smiled. She waddled back to the fruit section and took a moment to select me a replacement peach which she then gently placed in my basket, her crystal blue eyes sparkling up at me.

'Come on,' said the woman. Grabbing her by the arm, she whisked Mrs Crabtree up the aisle and away.

But then a curious thing happened. Just before she disappeared from view, Mrs Crabtree smiled back at me and winked. A very knowledgeable, worldly-wise wink.

Looking back, I don't believe this shrunken old lady was senile. I think she was an adventurer, making the most of the few remaining moments of adventure she had left. I planted the pip from the tiny Mrs Crabtree's peach. And after a few weeks, I had a tiny tree. Mrs Crabtree's Peach Tree. I thought of her every time I watered it. And I'm grateful she selected me to play a part in the adventure that was her life.

A PAIR OF CHERYLS

Eyelashes are funny things, aren't they? As a drag queen, I seemed to spend half my life plucking, shaving or tweezing one protrusion or another into submission. I didn't use hair removal creams because they brought me out in a rash. Another suggestion of rubbing up against the bark of a tree didn't hold too much appeal, though rubbing up against the drunken friend who suggested it was quite nice. But despite all the trouble us girls took to constantly vacate our follicles, when it came to eyelashes, the longer and thicker the better.

As my five-year-old niece had said to me not too long before, "When you dress up, the hair on your eyes looks pretty". Hairy eyes? Now there's a thing! But I suppose we should be grateful it's eye hair that's considered beautiful on a woman. Imagine hairy armpits in a peach chiffon evening gown? Or five o'clock shadow with coral pink Chanel lipstick? We'd all look like moosh-malts from Eastern Europe, and that would never do.

It was drag queen Mother Page who taught me how to stick on eyelashes with Copydex. I could never get on with the miniscule tube of adhesive supplied with every pair. At the time, I was performing eight shows a week. It was Summer and hot, and the sweat kept flushing my eye hair down the front of my face and into my cleavage. Help! Wood glue to the rescue. It keeps them on through wind, rain and riot but bleaches everything it touches, so not perfect. Now retired, I often wonder whether my natural lashes will ever return. Still, at the time it was cheap when you consider a tube could last a whole year. And twelve months of inconvenient bleaching was worth the misery just to see the embarrassed look on the face of the B&Q assistant's face when you told him what you wanted it for.

Travesty superstar Ron Storme told me to clean eyelashes in the palm of the hand with a spot of washing up liquid. Well if you could be arsed with all the faffing about it did make them last longer, but they still needed replacing now and then.

So it was that I headed off down the West End to get new ones. A visitor to my show had told me that pop group Girls Aloud had released their own range of eye hair. Apparently there was a different style for each aloud girl and they were well worth a look at. So there I was in Boots having a rummage in the "bits to stick on" aisle, when as if by magic Cheryl Cole's (or Tweedy, or Fernandez-Versini, or whatever her bloody name is today) adorable little face appeared from behind a box of gargantuan tampons that someone had been too embarrassed to take to the till and dumped in the wrong section. There was indeed a style for each member of the band. How marvellous! I pondered for a while why the ginger one's weren't ginger (no, I can't remember her name either) before finally settling for a pair of Cheryls.

Now, I'd not been in the Piccadilly Circus branch before and wasn't too sure where to pay. Down in the depths of the cellar as I was, I joined the back of a long queue for ten minutes before realising I was waiting among sick people collecting Swine Flu prescriptions. I threw a sensible hanky over my face and ran like buggery. It seemed my best option would be to go and find a till upstairs.

At the bottom of the steps, a rather austere security guard sprang out at me from behind a Factor Five display shouting, 'You cont!'

'I... I'm sorry?' I replied, trying frantically to think from where she would have known me.

'You cont teek them opstairs, you heff to pee for them doown here,' she shouted. I was acutely embarrassed to have not recognised she was speaking with a Nigerian accent. Thank heavens I'd questioned her and not just punched out. Sensible hanky held high and a little shaken, I returned to the sick people.

That evening in my dressing room, I laid all of my paraphernalia on the counter before me. On went the lippy, the rouge, the eye shadow and the eyebrows. Anticipation was building. I held hands with myself and said a pre-performance prayer - so Madonna!

'God bless the crew, sound, lighting, me... oh yes, and all the little orphan children,' (just in case Sir Cliff really was listening). Finally, with heightened anticipation and Copydex in hand, on went the Cheryls. I marvelled at the thick, succulent glamour of my new eye hair. Did I look like Miss Cole, as promised on the packet? Thirty grand of surgery and I might just make it!

SEVEN NOSES

Living in London's West End as I did at the time, I got to see and hear some funny things. Steeped in history with layers of time overlapping, things sprang out at you through the mists of time. It was a bit like being at the steam room on a Saturday night... you never know what's going to poke at you from out of the fog. So I suppose it wasn't really too much of a shock to be told about the legend that is The Seven Noses Of Soho.

A dear eccentric friend of mine who ran an Artistes Members Club nearby had told me that around the local streets were seven buildings, all of which had a nose. Well, being rather nosey myself, this was too exciting to ignore. So equipped with a camera, a notepad and a substantial amount of mountaineering equipment, off a group of us trotted to hunt them down.

After a couple of hours wandering around looking at buildings (well, shopping really), and several other distractions (a Justin Timberlake look-a-like sipping a cappuccino outside Compton's Café... we took turns from across the street with the binoculars), we decided to take our quest a little more seriously and split up.

I headed off to look at American retro burger bar Ed's Diner, a fabulous green and white corner-building near the east end of Old Compton Street. I stood across the road, staring up scanning every little nook and cranny. After a few moments I realised that a little group of tourists had gathered around me all looking in the same direction, trying to see what I was staring at. A woman across the street saw us but, rather than look up, she raised her umbrella as a precaution against something perhaps about to fall. Luckily for her it wasn't a huge chunk of loose masonry.

I decided to move on and double back into Romilly Street. Much to my amusement, my little group of tourists were still following me. Further more, another two or three had now tagged along. I felt like The Pied Piper in sling-backs. What delicious fun!

I shouted, 'Look out!' and the whole group of them ducked, covering the back of their heads with their hands. So I ran, and to my delight they ran after me. Not wanting to waste an opportunity, I legged it into my little pub. They followed and spent half an hour recovering from shock with a round of brandies from my till. Note to self - try this again! I did have rent to pay.

The next day, my phone rang at some God forsaken hour of the morning to tell me of a major breakthrough in our quest. Someone had found a nose! It took two cups of coffee and several cigarettes before I was in a fit state to wander out, but eventually I reached the spot. It was a small side turning off Dean Street called Meard Street. I looked up and sure enough on the side of the first building to the left was a nose. A large Streisandesque kind of conk, hanging over us from half-way up the wall.

I joined the little group that had gathered, all looking up at this shrine. Like the Holy Grail, for sad folk like me with nothing better to do on a Wednesday morning in Soho. What a surreal thing it was! We gazed in silent wonderment as though a vision of the Virgin Mary were floating there. We had a moment of light relief as a woman rushed by. Looking up at our fixation, she misjudged the corner altogether and bashed her own nose on the railings. Then someone in the group asked if Meard is the French word for shit. Knowing that Soho had a history of eighteenth-century European settlers, I wondered what this alley must have once been used for. My neck was aching now, so I headed back home for breakfast.

Not long after, another four of the seven noses were discovered. Nobody knew why they were there or what their purpose was. Could it have been a secret message; Soho's very own Da Vinci Code perhaps? Or something to do with The Freemasons? Would we ever find out? Most likely not. But where were the other two? Could it have been that there were now only five left? There was always a lot of renovation work taking place in Soho.

Anyway, I'd made a decision there and then that my little Soho pub should have its own nose. I would paint it with gold glitter to match my signage. And the eccentric friend who started the whole quest would get one too. One day we could go shopping and pick our noses together. Then Soho would once again have seven and all would be right with the world.

ADOLF THE WHELK

It had been one of those drag performances where everything seemed to go bloody wrong. The microphone was picking up intermittent signals from the local taxi firm, the crowd were being very arsey and, to top it all, I had a throat like a busy hooker. 'I must have been evil in a previous life,' I thought to myself.

On the long drive home, I began to wonder... if re-incarnation does exist, what could I have been before to come back as a drag queen? I had read somewhere that the more wicked a person is in one life, the lower the life form he or she will return as in the next. That said, drag was not a bad career. But it did have its share of horrors.

I was talking to my friend's neighbour Enid about this, as she seems to be up on these things. She sat there cross-legged on her sea-grass mat in her kaftan, with one hand on each knee meditating. She also had one breast on each knee but, as I understand it, hippies don't wear anything that restricts the flow of energy from one chakra to the other. Sitting just feet away from Enid, I assumed this included deodorant.

'You are here to consult my oracle?' she said in a mystic voice. Perhaps it was her oracle I could smell.

'Well, I just wanted to know about re-incarnation really,' I replied, turning my head sideways to quickly gasp a few mouthfuls of fresher air from behind me.

'Allow me to tune in to your aura. Relax and breathe deeply,' she instructed.

'I'm breathing as deeply as I can manage at the moment,' I coughed.

'Good... good... your aura is blue... with pink bits flashing,' she advised.

'Do I need to see someone about this?' I asked. It didn't sound normal to me.

'Just sit still and relax. I can re-adjust your nudus nexis from here.'

'With your eyes shut? That's very clever!'

She began swaying from side to side. 'The mists are clearing and I can see you in a big field with a big net.' I must have been a football player. Perhaps that's why I've got jippy knees. 'You have butterflies.' Probably pre-match nerves. 'You are catching them in your net. The year is... sixteen thirty. And you are a Queen.' No change there then.

'You are Elizabeth the First and you are in the gardens of Buckingham Palace.' You ought to watch The History Channel more often love, I thought to myself. The Palace wasn't built until seventeen thirty-two.

'No I don't need to know about me in a past life,' I explained. 'I just want to know more about how it all works.'

'Oh, why didn't you say so in the first place?' she said, snapping instantly out of her trance. 'You see, it's all a matter of karma. What you give, whether good or evil, you get returned tenfold. So, if you're really saintly like a nun or something, you'll come back rich and beautiful. But if you're a nasty bit o' work like Myra Hindley, you'll come back as a fish. That's how you learn your lesson.' Hmm. I was confused.

'But fish only have a three second memory. How can Myra Hindley learn her lesson if she comes back as a fish? Surely she'd have forgot about it by now.'

'Ah, but that's where karma's clever you see, 'cause it's all done automatically. All your doings are recorded in the Akashic Library in the great beyond for all to see.' I wasn't sure I liked the idea of all and sundry seeing my doings in the great beyond.

I still didn't really understand. I picked up my cup of tea for a swig to clear my throat, but all I could taste was oracle. I held it in my mouth for a moment till she turned to light a cigarette. Then I spat it behind one of the cushions on her shabby chaise.

'I sense you're confused,' she said. It sounded about the only thing she'd got right so far. 'Let me give you a good example. In our meditation circle last Tuesday, we got in touch with the essence of Adolf Hitler. He now lives on the coast of Cornwall.' That didn't sound too bad for a murderous dictator responsible for millions of horrific racist eliminations.

'Cornwall?'

'Yes Cornwall. He's a mollusc.' This was all getting a bit weird now, even for me.

'Mollusc?'

'Yes, he's a whelk. One of the lowest forms of life. Absolute proof that it doesn't pay to be evil. Then one day, he'll get caught and eaten in someone's paella and then he'll evolve into a slightly higher life-form next time around. Perhaps a pigeon, or lizard or something.'

'And what happens to the person who eats Adolf the whelk?'

'He or she will have it recorded in the Library that they contributed towards the retribution of the Jews.' Time to go, I thought. I'd planned to make a prawn salad for my partner Charlie's tea. Maybe he'd have been safer with beans on toast.

CATFORD TAN

'Looking pasty, Kristian,' I shrugged at myself in the mirror. It seems the older I got, the higher maintenance I became. I didn't used to have to pluck my nose. Or cut my toenails with dog clippers. Time for a little pampering, I thought. A deliciously rancid drag queen friend of mine suggested where to go for a cheap tan, diligently scrawling an address with eye pencil onto a bit of old toilet paper.

So with The Bahamas eluding me for yet another year, I headed for this place in Catford. And so it was I found myself in a car park facing a rather dilapidated concrete tower block. Wondering if Miss Rancid had had the last laugh here, I headed nervously for the lift. As I pressed what was left of the up button, it crossed my mind it was the kind of place I'd have expected to come for an abortion rather than a spray bronzing.

Arriving at the flat didn't change my first impressions.

'Hi, I'm Carol,' she squeaked. Over-tanned and hair bleached to within an inch of its life, she looked more like a photographic negative than a Beautician. 'Go through to the lounge. Sorry about the dog hair. Just make sure it don't stick to you when the spray's wet, it's a bugger to get off. D'ya wanna cup of tea?' There was a strange smell of wet Bull Mastiff and Woolworth's Number Six perfume.

'No, you're alright ta,' I replied with caution. I glanced around discreetly, checking for tell-tale knitting needles.

'Strip off and stand in that tent.' In an instant, my mind was back on location with the Boy Scouts...

Later, pondering my reflection in the steel lift doors, I became a bit concerned at how dark I looked. Still, at least it wasn't patchy. The mirror parted and I interrupted two round-bellied elderly ladies, mid-chatter. The screech of the doors closing made the ensuing silence even more deafening. I was wondering to myself whether the smell of piss was coming from the lift or my new travel companions. Then the one in the pink scarf started humming. I couldn't make out the tune... though I'm not sure it was one. Suddenly and desperately, the lift ground to a halt between floors.

'Don't worry love, it's always doing this. It'll start up again in a minute,' said the other one. I smiled my appreciation for her concern. Silence again. Then the old lady's humming turned to whistling. 'Stop whistling so loud. You might piss him off.'

A little taken aback by this granny's turn of phrase, I chuckle. 'It's fine, really.'

'What part of India you from with that accent then?' she asked, lifting her glasses to look closer at my new tan.

'Bermondsey,' I reply.

'Ooh, they got one of them over there too?'

Without warning, the lift plunged a short distance. As it jolted to a stop once more, the lights went out.

'Jesus H Christ,' one of them cried out in shock. My knees gave way and I banged my head on the lift wall. So there I was, alone in the dark with two senile old ladies… couldn't have been two hung tattooed skinheads, could it? I was sweating like Rolf Harris in a girl's school by this time.

'Ooh, it's just like the blackouts, ain't it?' said one. 'My old Mother was never happier than when the bombs were falling. Well, till that one landed on her head.'

'I don't think I ever saw your old mother without her hat on.' It was all getting a bit too surreal now, even for a drag queen like me.

'She never took it off. Indoors or out, even when she was in the tin bath in front of the fire.'

'Go on with yer!'

'No, seriously. Then of course that night she refused to go to the shelter. We told her, but she was happier in the cupboard under the stairs. Silly old cow. Course, the doodlebug landed right on top of her. When the firemen turned up, there was bits of her everywhere.'

I felt it only polite to join the conversation at this point. 'Did she still have her hat on?' I said, attempting to lighten the conversation a little. Icy silence. Oh dear!

The mobile toilet jolted into action again and the lights came back on. I decided never again to make eye contact with my old ladies. Though I did notice on the wall where I'd hit my head a rather runny looking brown stain. Fake tan… sweating… buggeration! I looked in the wing mirror of my car and there was a white patch in the middle of my forehead like Michael

Jackson. Then I noticed that my car aerial had been snapped off at the hip. Not such a cheap tan after all!

CASA MARIANNA

'Oh my God, we're going to crash into the sea!' I gulped, desperately hugging the back of the seat in front. That's exactly how it looked from the window of our plane because the landing strip was practically on the beach. The occupant of the seat in front was a heavily bejewelled and rather plump middle-aged woman. Rather upset that I'd also grabbed a large handful of her frizzy black hair in my frenzied state, she began waving her arms around and shouting at me in some native language or other. I handed back her now detached extensions and offered her a banana by way of a peace offering, but she took this as further insult and threw it up the back of the fuselage.

It was all rather stressful and equally embarrassing, so once we'd landed, I just wanted to get off and get to our Hotel. Though my partner Charlie and I were here to work a two-week season of my Diva Show and Cliff Richard Show, we had hoped to have a bit of a holiday at the same time. After that flight and what seemed like an age passing through the cattle-shed that was Lanzarote Airport, we needed this break more than ever.

Despite all of this our hosts were divine. Originally from the North of England, Brian and Rita had sold up and moved out here some years ago to start a new life in the sunshine. They met us at the airport and escorted us to their venue in the Old Town. They were well versed in the island's colourful history and folklore, and spent the journey excitedly sharing this learned wisdom. Charming though their enthusiasm was, it gave the impression they didn't get too many visitors. Trying to look interested was exhausting after such a difficult journey. Our first show would be that very night and we needed some rest. So having set out all the costumes in the dressing room, we were speedily delivered to where we would live for the duration of our stay - the fabled Casa Marianna.

From the main dust road, we climbed down a small flight of crooked stairs to a group of tiny white-washed villas. The windows and doors were all painted a faded sky blue. Terracotta roof tiles dulled the bright glare of sunlight a little, and an abundance of spiky green leaves pierced huge swathes of vivid red flowers. At the bottom of the steps was a small courtyard which opened onto a large sun-drenched paved area with a crystal-clear infinity pool overlooking the glittering ocean. At the back of the pool was a man-made waterfall. Chairs and sun loungers surrounded the water. It was breathtaking. We stood for a moment drinking it all in. Our fabulous holiday was about to begin!

'Magical, isn't it?' whispered Brian reverently. 'Ah, here comes Marianna now.' From behind a beaded door curtain across the patio stepped the frizzy haired woman from the plane. My heart sank. 'Marianna, this is Jeff and Charlie.'

'Hmm. We hayve met,' she spat. 'Disa way playze.' She spun on her heels and marched Charlie and I briskly to a ground floor room behind a set of double-glazed sliding patio doors. Without another word, she tossed a set of keys onto the bed and left. The room was barren and basic and smelled like a locker room at a college gym - under any other circumstances, probably quite acceptable in a testosterone-soaked kind of way. The wardrobe had a door missing and only three coat hangers. The toilet was a hole in the floor.

'Jesus Christ,' whinged Charlie. 'It looks like somewhere you'd be held hostage!' He was right. Was this about budget or revenge? Or worse still, some kind of latent karma? We decided to leave the patio doors wide open to air the room and have a much-needed snooze on the attached veranda. Unfortunately as we slept, our shaded area became a suntrap, so I did my first Lanzarote show with severe sunstroke. But worse was to come. Upon returning to the villa late that night, our room was literally as hot as an oven. It dawned on us that the only ventilation was through the sliding patio doors. We could either spend the night slowly roasting with the doors closed or leave them open and have our throats cut while being robbed as we slept. Either way, we'd probably be dead by morning.

'Let's just lock up the bags and sleep on the terrace where it's cooler,' suggested Charlie. Sounded like our best option.

I awoke to brilliant sunshine after just about four hours sleep, with a huge ragged chicken pecking disconcertedly at my flip-flop. Not only did we still have sunstroke and exhaustion from the day before, but we were now both covered in mosquito bites and sunburnt down one side of our face, one arm and one leg. It was in this state of surreal shock we wandered out into town to find some food, only to discover it was siesta and everything would be shut for a few hours. Like vestiges of The Empire, we smiled graciously through our stiff upper-lips without complaint, while somewhat politely and rather Britishly hobbling back to Casa Marianna. Just thirteen more bastard days to go…

KING KONG

My gorgeous little pub in Soho was a very old lady. She was born in 1731 and subsequently, like all of us as we get a bit older, needed a lot of maintenance. But finding a tradesman willing to work in Soho was not an easy task, what with extortionate parking costs and the thieving Congestion Charge. You couldn't even step out of a parked van without some rookie traffic warden creeping up on you like a rash. I'm not sure even Anneka Rice would have coped with the challenge. So you can imagine my delight to discover that one of my regular patrons had been shagging a plumber. Normally customers are only too pleased to introduce me to a good contact, but on this occasion my patron was a little evasive. This is rather odd, but when a girl needs a new u-bend! Several rather large whiskies later, a meeting was arranged.

The next morning a huge hirsute hulk of a man arrived with a clipboard. Ape like with arms hanging down past his knees, he had more hair on his fingers than he did on his head. It was a bit of a shock at first, having just watched King Kong the night before. Suddenly I was Fay Wray hanging off the Empire State Building in sugar pink moleskin mules.

I stood there in the shadow he cast across the entire bar, wondering how he was going to fit under my little sink with his monkey wrench. Then from out behind him sprang my patron, who I previously hadn't noticed.

'This is Mister Mike,' he said sheepishly.

'Shut up and sit down!' growled Mister Mike. Instantly he responded by sitting cross-legged on the floor. For a moment I wasn't sure whether I was also supposed to be sitting on the floor. This led me to bob slightly, almost like a vague attempt at a curtsy. However, the estimate began and I was off the hook. My joke about falling in the sink while tap dancing fell on deaf ears, but a deal was struck and I finally had my elusive plumber. And any fear of him not fitting under my sink was of no consequence as his arms were long enough to reach the cellar floor from the top of the stairs.

Two days later, I got a phone call from my patron. He asked me to go and collect the estimate from an address in Lewisham. I'd have expected it to come through the post or email. However it did seem like a good opportunity to do a bit of shopping, and to do lunch with my old drag mucker The Duchess, at her duchy The George And Dragon on the outskirts of Deptford (she calls it Greenwich, who am I to argue?)

Having caught up on all the vicious gossip, I headed for The Empire State Building to collect my estimate from Kong. He opened the door wearing nothing but a pair of leather trousers with Doc Martins. The rest of him was a mass of hair and fat, like four large dogs sewn together and not smelling much better.

'Go through there,' he said pointing to a door at the end of the long hallway. I entered what looked like the bondage stockroom at Clone Zone. There were whips, chains, hammocks and slings and a long shelf to one wall with a row of about thirty dildos in every size, shape and colour one could imagine. From a small CD player to one side, I could hear monks humming Abba's song S.O.S. To another wall was a pin board covered with polaroids of men in one form of compromise or another. I'm not a girl that's easy to shock, but a bit of warning might have been nice!

Suddenly from one dark corner there was a muffled choking sound, like someone trying to speak with a mouth full of Cornish Pasty… I was reminded of my lunch with The Duchess. Then through the gloom I noticed my patron, hanging upside down strapped to what looked like a crucifix bejewelled with black and gold rhinestones. He was naked wearing nothing but a gag and what could only be described as a designer mousetrap on his rather red and swollen looking bell end. My first instinct was to laugh. Then it occurred to me that I hadn't yet discovered why I'd been sent in there to collect my estimate.

I removed the gag. 'What the fuck's going on?' I enquired politely.

'Oh, he's printed out an estimate for the job and if it's OK, he can start Tuesday morning at seven thirty. Is that alright?'

I hastily collected my estimate and left. By return of post, I sent an invoice for taking part in Kong and the patron's humiliation game. Needless to say, nobody arrived Tuesday morning. Anyone know a plumber?

MYSTIC TULIP

Many moons ago, I used to tarot read at Psychic and Mystic Fayres. With my long wavy hair, kaftan and crystal ball I used to do quite well on my glitzy little table in the corner of the hall. Upon arrival, I'd set out all me paraphernalia on a silken cloth. Then go buy a loaf of bread to feed the local pigeons to bring myself good luck for the day, a routine a fellow reader from Pakistan had taught me. All very Mary Poppins. It was this man who suggested I might benefit from a Mystic Wonder Weekend on this farm in Cheshire. A couple of days communing with nature among the cows and chickens sounded like a nice idea at the time. With no clue as to what young farmers were wearing that season, I threw a pair of Jesus sandals and a couple of clean pairs of drawers in a knapsack and headed into the sunrise.

Upon arrival, the idyllic Darling Buds of May farmyard I had imagined throughout my journey was not the reality. Instead, in front of me were three modern pre-fabricated huts on a big slab of concrete in the middle of a sun-scorched field. They reminded me of the chemistry classrooms at school, just far enough up the playing field that any explosion wouldn't take out the main building, more's the pity.

With a sigh I headed towards a sign that said 'Enter The Realm Of The Nymphs', written with biro on a chunk of cornflake packet card. Daffodil met me at the door - a beamy man with a bald shiny cranium and tufted grey beard. He looked like he had his head on upside down. He was wearing what appeared to be last season's Laura Ashley floral curtains tied into a Ghandi-esque nappy, held with a giant kilt pin. As he folded my hundred-pound cheque into four and shoved it into his waistband, he explained that here in Mother Nature's bosom we all exchange our own names for that of a flower.

After getting my head around the bosom thing, I deliberated over the possibilities of Bindweed, Poison Ivy and African Bird Eating Orchid before finally settling on Tulip.

Hut number two, rather optimistically re-named as The Rainbow Fairy Grove was to be my sleeping place for the night, the rest of the time to be spent in lessons and meditation in The Realm Of The Goblin, otherwise known as the woods round the back of the huts. The Rainbow Fairy Grove stunk of body odour and bad breath, so I dumped my Louis Vuitton and headed to The Realm Of The Goblin in the hope it was as Hampstead Heath as it sounded.

On the edge of the wood stood a large oak tree. A naked heavy breasted woman was clinging to it possessively. 'I really love you, tree.' she shouted, desperately. The tree didn't answer, and I wondered which poor beau from her past it was substituting for. Suddenly without warning, a small skinny bespectacled man wearing lilac fairy wings with matching thong flitted up to me.

'Hello, I'm Pansy, what's your name?' he asked excitedly, flapping his wrist tied wings.

'Tulip, mate,' I said.

'What a lovely name! You have chosen wisely. Come hither among the fauna.' And away he flapped.

'Be there in a bit,' I replied, walking in the opposite direction.

My cabaret shows regularly had visitors of all colours, creeds, nationalities, shapes and sizes wearing every sort of combination you could shake a stick at. No problem. But this was something else! I sat on a small precipice overlooking a sparkling stream. On the opposite bank was a very agitated old lady trying to set light to a small pile of damp leaves by banging together a rock and a bit of old hoof. In her frustration, she shrieked a stream of obscenities at this innocent little pile of foliage. I tried to justify in my mind why I would find visitors to my show being eccentric acceptable and yet the nymphs of this realm not so. My attention focused back to the frustrated little old lady, who by this time was close to tears and bashing her pile of leaves with a big stick. I think that, like the woman with the tree, perhaps the gentle folk here were attempting to find something rather than be something. Maybe searching in an alien environment had an appeal because it enabled them to not have to face their own reality in their own environment. Luckily for me, I'm happy with my own reality, so I decided that my search was going to be for the bus stop home to my own environment… before Daffodil had had time to cash my fuckin' cheque!

FINNIGAN'S CARDIGAN

Much to my dismay, the time had finally come. I'd had to have CCTV cameras fitted in my little Soho pub. It wasn't the cost that bothered me, though of course I'd rather have bought jewellery. Molly's was the smallest cabaret pub in Soho, so I didn't need much equipment. It was the invasive nature of the bastard things I didn't like. Someone told me at the time that, being a drag queen, I should have enjoyed being photographed and filmed. Well as they say, any publicity is good publicity. But CCTV cameras are a different lipstick altogether; designed to spy and watch rather than glamorise and publicise. They don't even capture you with good lighting, which at my age could be a problem in itself.

Thieving buggery traffic cameras are bad enough, and a bane to anyone in my profession. Driving around the country from show to show in drag or otherwise, it doesn't matter how much time you give yourself to reach any given destination, there'll always be sufficient road works forcing you to rush the last bit of your journey. And I don't care what anyone says, if they were about slowing you down rather than generating income, they wouldn't all be so bloody small and hidden in fucking treetops or behind traffic signs. That said my real horror is CCTV in shopping precincts. I recall a drama of mine from a few years ago.

Winter was coming and, having just spent my lunch watching Judy Finnigan in a hideous pink and white fluffy wrap-around, it occurred to me that I myself may also need to update my wardrobe. So there I was fingering a jumper in Primarni when I suddenly felt a judder down my left leg. It was a bit of a shock because I'd only just worked out how the vibrate function on my mobile worked and wasn't yet used to its impromptu, yet not unpleasant attack on my sensibilities. It was a text. "You're too fat to wear that". I was mortified! I didn't recognise the number it was sent from and looking around, I couldn't see anyone I knew. I threw the garment back on the rail and went instead to search for a new pair of jeans.

Another text. "Lard arse jeans are at the back". I dropped the jeans on the floor and ran out of the store. In the coffee shop next door, I ordered a latte to calm my nerves.

"Hope that's a skinny". I nearly dropped the fucking thing.

I texted back, "who is this?!"

"Ha! ha!" came the reply. Rattled, I spilt my coffee down the front of my coat. "Sloppy!" I ran out and up the precinct walkway to the escalator. This invasion on my privacy was too much... I'd not long recovered from the shock of Finnigan's cardigan.

I hurried to the wide row of exits. The middle door was locked. I tried another door and likewise couldn't get out. Nobody else seemed to be having trouble, just me. As I rushed to another door, I heard the click of an automatic lock. I stood bewildered for a moment or two not really knowing what to do for the best – perhaps a bit like Richard and Judy's wardrobe mistress. Who do I have to shag to get out of this place?

Then a door marked private swung open and out leapt a uniformed security guard. 'I'm sorry Mr Kristian, I'm afraid I'm going to have to frisk you.' Had he looked like Colin Farrell in his SWAT gear rather than Sergeant Bilko, I might have considered the prospect interesting. But this stranger knew my name and my mobile number, which was a bit disconcerting.

'Do I know you? How do you know my number?' I asked suspiciously.

'It's me... Tommy,' he laughed. 'You know... I used to book your show at Bubbles in Deptford.'

'I'm not happy, Tommy,' I scolded.

'Oh, I was only having a laugh,' he replied sarcastically, gesturing to a CCTV camera. The door lock clicked open and I left. Perhaps by this time I was paranoid, but even the car park cameras appeared to be following my apparently lard arse. It was unnerving.

Being on camera professionally is one thing. Because you've got time to prepare (Ms Finnigan must have been late on set that morning). Even with reality shows like Big Brother, you know what you're letting yourself in for. But it comes to something when you can't even pick your arse in the street without knowing whether or not it'll be on YouTube by Friday. Bloody CCTV... you just don't know who's watching!

LOLLIPOPS AT DAWN

At school my careers advisor asked what I wanted to do for a living, and I told her, 'I want to be a Lollipop Man.' When she asked why, I told her it appealed to me that I wouldn't have to start working until I was sixty-five. This was of course a joke, though at the time the miserable old goat didn't see the funny side.

Our lollipop lady was a sparkling gem. Known endearingly as Old Vera, she would be there to greet us cheerily every morning and then again every evening through wind, rain and earthquake in that canary-coloured tabard with the bit hanging and those fur lined booties. One day without warning, she wasn't there anymore and for some time our entire school was thrown into disarray. No more big round smiley face. No more Quality Street at Easter and Christmas. She was just gone and we missed her.

Some considerable years later, I was booked to perform at a working man's club in Hull. I was shown to the dressing room... well, a large cupboard under the stairs basically. There was a chunk of old mirror propped atop a stack of tatty municipal chairs. And what appeared to be a ten-watt light bulb hanging bare from a rather lethal looking bit of cobwebbed wire, looped by a hook from a hole in the corner of the ceiling. Having only two weeks beforehand to prepare for a show in Bradford at the top of piss-stained concrete steps next to a puddle of sick, I counted my blessings and began to unpack my kit bag. Leaning across the chairs and a little in front of the mirror was a traffic lollipop. In an instant my mind flashed back to Old Vera. With a smile, I picked it up and moved it across the room by the door out of the way. Such a familiar object, and yet I'd never before handled one. I was surprised at how little it weighed. I struggled to put on my makeup in the dull glow from the dusty bulb, trying desperately not to end up looking like an elderly Barbara Cartland.

Suddenly the door flew open and in marched a short militant looking woman with a hairdo that looked like it had been commissioned by Hull Borough Council. With a huff and a puff, she picked up the lollipop and placed it back in front of me against the chairs, once again half blocking the mirror. Then without a word, she turned on her heals and left, slamming the door behind her. As the door slammed, the lollipop slipped knocking the mirror, which fell from the chair and smashed on the floor at my bare stockinged feet.

I stood for a moment in bewilderment. I was just counting to check all my toes were still attached, when once again the door flew open and in rolled the red-faced Chairman of the club's committee.

'You can't come in here tampering with other people's property,' he growled at me. 'And to top it all, you've broken our mirror.'

'Eh?' I was to say the least confused.

'You've been meddling with our Ivy's lollipop and it's got to stop or we'll have a riot on our hands.' A riot over a lollipop? In an instant, Ivy was back.

'I've told you Vernon, I'm not going stand for it. I've got special permission from The Borough and you've no right move it. I'm on medication. I'll have my say again with the committee on Monday, you see if I don't.'

'But Ivy, I've told you it wasn't me in the car that night. She couldn't have been the one.' It was like some sort of low budget soap on cable telly, the kind you can only watch when stoned.

'I'm sorry love, I only moved it out of the way of the mirror,' I intervened.

'Don't "love" me, I'm nobody's love.' she scowled.

'Yes, I can see why,' I replied. She grabbed the lollipop and swung it towards my head. I ducked and there was a bright flash and loud bang as she missed me and took out the light bulb.

'Now look what you've made me go and do!' She began sobbing. In silhouette against the light of the corridor, I could see Vernon pull her against him.

'Now Ivy love, don't go getting yourself all upset again. It was all a long time ago. Come on, I'll get you a cup of tea.' They left and closed the door behind them.

So there I was. Semi-naked in a pitch-dark cupboard, half made-up, surrounded by shards of broken glass. I never did learn Ivy's apparently traumatic story. In the calm after the storm, my mind returned to Old Vera. Why did she suddenly disappear? It didn't occur to us kids that she might have a life away from the crossing. I'm sure Ivy's kids hadn't considered hers either.

FAREWELL MANKY

'Look at him staring at you,' taunted Rita from next door. 'He's got hollow eyes, like a stalker.'

'Don't be ridiculous!' I replied.

'Yes, but don't it bother you that he's sitting there listening to every word you say?'

'I'm used to it,' I said. 'Remember it was only yesterday you was leaning over your balcony two floors up, craning your neck to hear my phone conversation through my kitchen window.'

'I was reaching for a cobweb. Anyway, I thought I heard you say you'd got a pet monkey.'

'His name's Manky and anyone can see he's a pigeon, you silly bitch,' I said. Manky stared back at us blankly from his position on the hearthrug.

Rita continued, 'Only, my Great Aunt had a pet monkey and it kept masturbating over the velour plush.'

A fortnight earlier, I'd been taking down the nets to the French doors of my own balcony. I was amazed to see a mother pigeon nesting a single egg in one of my window boxes. Manky hatched, but after a few days Mother of Manky was gone, never to return. Her poor bedraggled offspring just sat there. I was worried. I put out some dry crusts of bread on a saucer but he wouldn't touch it. That night it rained. I put my peg bag over him to keep him dry. Later, I noticed he was eating the soggy bread, so I put out some more soaked in milk, which he seemed to like. When I hooked the peg bag back on my line, suddenly he was gone. I was happy he'd found his strength.

Later that night, I'd been watching The Two Ronnies for nearly an hour before I notice Manky sitting under the telly table staring back up at me... he must have come in when I had the door open. He soon settled in. A week later he was sat on my lap watching The Two Ronnies with me. I tried to vary his food from bread and milk to break his routine. I bought him a cuttlefish, though he didn't know what to do with it. I gave him some Trill but he couldn't keep it on the saucer. Then he tried to peck it off the floor, but he got his beak caught in the carpet loops. Most of the time he just sat there staring at me... vacantly.

'It's cause he thinks you're his Mother,' said Rita.
'You ought to stop feeding him.'
'I heard it's lucky to feed pigeons.'
'Anyway, how do you know he's a boy?' Hmm. I thought for a moment. I'd kind of just assumed he was. 'Has he got a penis? Pick him up and have a look.' I was curious now. I picked him up and held him aloft. He looked down at me and cooed.
'No, nothing,' I said, putting him back in front of the fire.
'Do you think roast pigeon would taste like chicken?' said Rita cruelly. 'Only I've got some frozen pastry in the freezer.'
'You evil witch!' I said, but she was undeterred.

'In the war, my Granddad used to go to Trafalgar Square with a sack and bring pigeons home for dinner.'

'That's vile! Anyway, I thought they evacuated all the pigeons during the war?' I was sure I'd read that somewhere.

'Oh don't be daft,' she said. 'Imagine the chaos trying to get three thousand pigeons on a train to Cornwall.'

'And you said your Grandfather was in Italy during the war.'

'That was my other Granddad fighting in Boulogne.'

'That's France… how many Granddad's did you have?'

'Oh I don't know, do I? We only ever go to Skegness!' She paused for another sip of tea. 'Anyway, you ought to get that thing out of the house, it's not healthy. People can catch things from pigeons. And they're not lucky. You see them walking around town with feet missing and bits hanging off. Can't it fly away yet?'

'I'm not sure.'

'Well there's one way to find out, throw it over the balcony.' She was void of all compassion but she did have a point. Would he ever want to fly if he was stuck indoors? I gently picked him up and on a count of three launched him into the air. He dropped like a stone, bounced off the sofa and disappeared down the back of a cushion.

'Oh my God, I've killed him!' I screamed, launching the cushion into the air behind me. But he was fine… just sitting there looking as bewildered as ever, if not perhaps a bit more manky than before.

Several days later, I could hear a clicking noise and I couldn't figure out what it was. Finally, I realised it was Manky sitting behind the net curtains pecking at the glass on the French doors. A little wave of sadness flushed over me. Perhaps this was it. Perhaps it was time for my surrogate baby to fly the nest. I took a deep breath and opened the door. Hopping out, he looked around and flapped his wings a little. He was determined to fly, though on his first attempt he hit his head on my peg bag and fell back down again. But it only took him seconds to pluck up courage and launch graciously into the air. He flew across to a clump of trees in the middle of the grass courtyard, returning to the balcony a few moments later and cooing at me. 'There's a clever boy!' I encouraged. Then he soared again, stopping briefly on the roof opposite to glance back. 'Farewell Manky. Be lucky, my darling.' And then he was gone.

DATING FLORRIE

We were having trouble trying to decide the age of a dear, yet rather plastically-altered friend of ours. For the purpose of this story, we'll call her Florrie. Of course, in an anti-ageist world, one shouldn't openly discuss these things. But she's such an old cow that we couldn't resist. Don't get me wrong... I'm absolutely one hundred per cent behind the notion of always attempting to look one's best. There's a plethora of trashy magazines oozing with photos of one celebrity or another with their face so pulled back that it looks as though they've just parachuted off an emergency evacuation flight from Afghanistan. And what about those Downing Street doorstep shots of Cheri Blair... when she answered her own front door (bless her) the morning after her husband's election victory? In this Facebook age of too much information, it's elegant for a woman of substance to retain some mystique. But when it came to Florrie, we were still desperate to know just how fucking old she really was!

'Cut off her head and count the rings!' someone screamed. Of course, it's now a well-known historical fact that this is what really started The French Revolution. We'd even considered hacking a bit of her off and sending it for carbon dating. The problem with this is that you've got to know which bits are still original and Gawd alone knows which bits of Florrie still are.

On one occasion, my friend Sandra detained her at the front door while I climbed in the back window to go through the linen cupboard in the hope of another Turin Shroud. The closest I could find was something with an odd-looking stain in her knickers drawer. Unfortunately it pulled out half the drawer lining with it. Then on my way back to the lab (Sandra's very own Girl Guide Home Chemistry Set) it mysteriously went missing, somewhere between the bus stop and my visit to the chip shop (after squirting my hands with a bit of Dettol spray). Many Holy relics from ancient times have indeed vanished without trace, so perhaps a clue to authenticity but still no help with dating our own not-so-holy relic.

'Has anybody actually asked her?' said a tetchy neighbour, desperate to change the subject.

So it was, Sandra and I invited Florrie for coffee one sunny April afternoon. We suggested we'd meet in Nero's, but it soon became clear that nothing short of a liquid lunch at Claridge's would net the old shark.

'We just had to meet you today because it occurred to us that we'd missed your birthday last year,' came my vague attempt at opening dialogue. Florrie smiled… well it was sort of an attempted smile through Botox. A side-glance to Sandra told me she'd also clocked how Florrie's ears moved more during this attempt than her mouth actually did.

'Darlings, how sweet,' she replied sourly, managing to motor her bottom lip just enough for the words to exit. I also noticed how her head never turned. She just batted her eyes from side to side occasionally to check out passing jewellery. It was like having lunch with Thunderbird puppet Lady Penelope, though Florrie didn't look as human.

'How many years is it this year?' I asked casually, taking a sip of my Lapsang Souchong.

'Darling I never discuss age, not even with my dear, dear friends.'

'Yeah but you can tell us, can't ya?' said Sandra, wincing as I kicked her under the table.

'Erm... would you like an iced fancy?' I was desperate now, if not intrigued to see how she'd get it in her gob.

'No thank you darling I don't have much time. I have to go straight to Heathrow from here. I'm jetting off to... Monaco... for a party. I just need to pop to the little girl's room.' As she rose stiffly and left the table, it seemed we had failed.

'Monaco?' gasped Sandra. 'Poland more likely, to get something that didn't stay in place stitched back on!'

'Wait a minute...' I said. The mists of an idea were clearing. 'Going straight to Heathrow? She'll be carrying her passport!'

By the time Florrie returned to our table, we had it all worked out. I'd keep her talking while Sandra pinched her handbag and took it to the loo for a rummage. But by mistake the silly bitch took the bag of a neighbouring diner, so we got thrown out.

Sandra phoned me later that night and told me how she'd been feeling ill and flushed since Claridges. It wasn't until she had a bath a few hours later that she'd realised she had an HRT patch stuck to the front of her wrist. It must have been loose in the handbag she'd ransacked. So we still don't know Florrie's vintage. But one thing I am sure of... I'm not going to grow old worrying about it.

CUCKOO CRAWFORD

A friend had asked me what my next New Year's Resolution would be. Apparently, she had decided she was going to give up smoking. This was after having already told me she was going to spend the festive season with her parents. What a load of old bollocks! She would need forty fags and back up drugs just for the journey home from Christmas with the family. The trouble is, it's the time of year when we're all thrown together by tradition, in one confined space as though we actually like each other. It's just not natural.

But from experience, I can say with some authority that there is something worse than spending Christmas with your family. Something much, much worse. And that's spending it with someone else's. Once all the usual inter-blood bitchiness and pickiness is over and everyone's sick of Turkey fuckin' sandwiches, boredom sets in and the cuckoo in the nest become the target. As I discovered to my horror when I attended a different friend's family home for my festive lunch.

He had told me that all his family do fancy dress at Christmas, which I thought sounded like fun. But upon arrival I discovered that by Fancy Dress, he actually meant they wear Sunday Best. So there they all were, around the dinner table in their favourite TopMan jacket and trousers or Marks and Spencer pastel two-piece. And there was I, Guest of Honour at the head of the table in a long black and pink sequinned ball gown as Joan Crawford. Not a good start. Then as a huge plate stacked high with dead bird arrived in front of me, it transpired that my gorgeous friend has also forgotten to pre-warn his Mum that I don't eat meat. That was before discussions even began on the dangers of eating Brussels sprouts while wearing thirty denier dance tights. Too much farting and your ankles swell up like water retention.

After sharing my dinner out amongst the other diners, I was obliged to eat an extra-large portion of equally disgusting sherry trifle. Granny smiled, affirming this was by way of an apology, despite whinging loudly from the kitchen while checking the back of the packet to ensure the jelly was made from pectin and not gelatine. But the look on Mum's face told the real motive for forcing me to eat too much pudding... revenge! Then it was on to the party games. Despite announcing I now felt a little sick, it had been decided we would start with a family tradition - the glorious Charades. As I was in costume, I must go first. And of course, I must do something with Joan Crawford in it, otherwise it wouldn't make sense. The problem was, the only film they all knew from our Joanie was Whatever Happened to Baby Jane, so I only got one turn. This would have been a blessing in disguise, were it not for having to sit through all the usual mimes... Jaws, Gone With the Wind, Titanic, Debbie Does Dallas...

Then family tradition reared its ugly head again as we all sat huddled together on the three-piece to watch One Of Our Dinosaurs Is Missing. I was close to tears by this time. 'Don't be sad,' Granny said, 'they get the dinosaur back at the end.'

'Imagine trying to get a Turkey as big as that in the oven,' Mum joked bitterly, with a dark glance in my direction. Sensing tension, Dad decided to try making me more comfortable by striking up conversation.

'So Jeff, did you see Man U take out Arsenal on Saturday?' If despair had a middle name, it would at that moment have been Jeff.

Suddenly my mobile phone rang. My mood brightened for a moment, if only for the irony of my I Will Survive ring tone. It was actually a wrong number; someone trying to find out if their local Chinese takeaway was open, but I seized the moment.

'Oh my God, no!... Where did they get run over?... Accident and Emergency?... I'll be right there.' I jumped to my feet in fake distress. 'I'm so sorry, it's my Aunt. She's been run over. Oh what a shame, just when I was getting to know you all.'

Mum piped in, 'Hope she didn't miss her Turkey.' Yeah alright love, let it go! Granny dived head first into the pile of duffle coats and cagoules to retrieve my full-length white fake fur wrap with coordinated French pink tassels.

So that New Year, there was a resolution for me. I wasn't going to fuck about trying to stop smoking or lose weight. But I did try to spend more quality time with my own family. Because despite all the trauma and dilemma at Christmas, or any other time of the year, better the devil you know!

DORIS AND BERT

Sometimes you've just got to get away from the hustle and bustle of routine day-to-day life for a few hours. So it was that my partner Charlie and I decided to lock the office, jump in a cab and just disappear.

'Where d'ya wanna end up?' said the Cabbie, taking another bite of his sandwich.

'Somewhere cheap!' yelled Charlie before I had a chance to put my mouth in gear. It wasn't a long journey before we arrived at the glorious Victoria and Albert Museum in Knightsbridge; free entry, donations on the door.

The place was vast. We stood in awe for a moment in the entrance lobby, as did a coach party of little elderly wrinkled folk. One remarked to his wife, 'Their heating bill must be big, Doris.'

I giggled. 'Could you imagine if Queen Victoria had been called Doris?' I said to Charlie. 'Queen Doris... how camp is that? We'd be visiting the Doris and Albert Museum.'

'Doris and Bert,' he added. Suddenly the austerity of the Victorian Gothic interior lightened when reconsidered as "Doris Gothic". And the list is endless. You could return home by train from Doris Station at Doris, to be warmed in front of your cast-iron Doris fireplace in the front room of your Doris terraced house. Or catch the bus along Doris Embankment... I'm even boring myself with it now! Still, the museum ahead of us looked promising.

We'd heard a rumour that Princess Di's Wedding Dress was on display here. So I grabbed a floor plan and we headed into the depths. First came a hall of statues. There was one of a woman crying. One of two men fighting. Another of a man chained to a rock.

'This is fucking depressing!' said Charlie. I had to agree. Through a giant doorway was a great hall of oriental things... and then more statues.

'I need a toilet,' I said.

'I need a fag,' said Charlie. Out came the floor plan. But the writing was so small that I couldn't actually read it. We decided to follow the smell of coffee... if there was a Café, there must be a loo. Thankfully there was, so Charlie grabbed a drink while I had a piddle. Then, after almost being knocked off our feet by a youth running through the Great Hall of Plastic Things, we happened upon yet more statues. 'Is these the same statues as before or is these other statues?' asked Charlie, trying to sound enthusiastic.

'Not sure,' I replied. 'Look for a man chained to a rock.'

'Hmm,' said Charlie. 'I'm sure that one there had a bigger cock the last two times we came through.'

'Perhaps he was pleased to see you the first two times. Now he's just bored.'

'I know how he feels,' said Charlie. 'Let's try upstairs.'

At the top of the third flight, we had to stop for breath. We'd probably walked about three miles by this time and my sciatica was kicking in. In front of us atop a pedestal was yet another statue, this time a bust of Doris herself.

'Is that the one they used to kill Archie in The Queen Doris pub on Eastenders?' asked Charlie. Through yet another great hall of old things, we were beginning to give up hope of ever finding this fuckin' wedding dress. Then finally I saw a sign pointing towards the Hall of Textiles.

'That's it!' my cry echoed up the hall. Two tourists leaped from an adjoining alcove, cameras poised desperate not to miss anything. They seemed quite rattled when they realised they hadn't.

Finally, we reached the costumes. They ran in chronological order from about seventeen-hundred to date. 'Look at this Charlie.' It's a huge bustled silk gown in a dull sage green. Probably the sort of thing Doris herself would have worn. 'God, I'm glad women don't wear that now. If I had to dress like that for my drag show, I'd be sweating like some wild farm animal.' We had a good laugh, but the tables were soon turned when we reach the nineteen-seventies. Two young students were pointing and laughing at a brown velvet suit with big lapels and flared trousers, topped off with a paisley shirt and two-tone platform shoes. Charlie looked devastated.

'What's the matter, darling?' I asked.

'I used to wear a suit exactly like that!' he cringed. The students turned and asked if they can take a photo of us "museum exhibits" with their iPhone. Hmm. So we're sorry for taking the piss out of your museum Doris and Bert. In a funny sort of way, we did actually have a lovely afternoon!

OFF TO OZ

When it comes to medical things, I'm not particularly squeamish. I don't have any kind of morbid fascination, but many a time I've sat in front of the telly with a bag of vegetarian wine gums and watched someone being probed with a spatula while having some piece of their anatomy or other fiddled with. Even blood and guts don't bother me. However, following some stomach pain, I was a little disconcerted when told I needed to have a camera inserted. 'We just need to take a little look up there,' said the Doctor.

'You might as well, everyone else has,' said my friend Carmen, who'd come along for moral support. After several side remarks about how many of the camera crew would be accompanying the camera, a date was set.

The morning of my appointment, I was starving. Not being allowed to eat or drink anything for twelve hours prior may as well have been twelve days. I think it was the knowing I couldn't eat that made me want to all the more. Carmen had agreed to drive me, though God alone knows why I asked her after our previous visit. But I was going to be sedated, so would need someone to get me home. I was collected from reception by a rather fit looking Australian in a pale blue scrub outfit. In his sexy accent, he of course called me Jiff. Carmen commented, 'like the toilet cleaner,' but I think she was just jealous it wasn't her being probed. I was led into a small anti room, where the Australian stud told me to strip and put on a gown. A cheap white cotton thing tied at the back with strings, not the full-length billowing sequinned numbers I was used to. I was then led into a larger room that looked more like the sterile operating theatres I had seen on telly. I was delighted to discover that there was yet another tanned Australian thing at my disposal… maybe they'd got a job lot? How do they get their teeth so fuckin' white? The thought did cross my mind for a moment that they may be Job Experience boys, which was a bit worrying. But my mind cleared of all other things when he walked towards me with a long stick topped with a brass hook. 'Jesus! What are you going to do with that?' I cried.

'Open the extractor vent,' he laughed, putting a reassuring hand on my shoulder.

'Hop up on the bench and lay on your side,' said the first. I did but, as I turned, I came eye to eye with an Asian man wearing Nana Mouskouri glasses and a comb-over. At first I thought he was kneeling down, but then I realised he was just very short.

'Hello Jeffrey,' he said quietly, peering at me over the top of his Nana's. He had a strange, unnerving calmness about him, like Notting Hill strangler John Christie. 'I'm going to sedate you now. You will feel a small prick.' I glanced over at the two beach buddies grinning back at me. I didn't imagine either of them to have a small prick, and I doubted the doctor could reach from down there. Suddenly I was floating and happy and everything seemed rather sexy.

And the doctor seemed somehow taller. I'm not sure if it was the drug or if he was now standing on a box.

'We will be able to see everything on this TV monitor. You can watch if you want to, or you can turn to face me.' I decided to watch the screen.

My memory of the next hour is rather vague, but there are a few poignant moments I do remember. As I watched the monitor, I saw the camera approach and commented that I'd never seen myself from that angle before. 'Now I know how it feels for porn stars,' I mumbled to the laughter of the two scrubs, who through a haze of sedation had now taken on a look of porn stars themselves. I also remember commenting that I couldn't feel the camera and had they considered getting one in a larger size. The very last thing I recall is commenting that I wasn't in Kansas anymore. That I was probably in Oz... and that at that moment I quite fancied a bit of Oz in me.

Their laughter was still echoing in my ears when I came round in a small white recovery room. Carmen was sitting at my side fingering through a copy of Hello. 'Alright?' I asked. She threw the magazine on the floor and scowled at me through her North Beach Cockle sunglasses.

'This is the one and only time I ever do this for you. I'm not a prude, but I've never been so embarrassed.'

'Eh?' I was confused. Then Australian number-one poked his head through the curtain.

'All done, you can go now Jiff,' he laughed... rather too hysterically for comfort. I just smiled graciously and gave a little wave.

I was still a little swimmy in the head on the car journey home, so the bitter stony silence was actually a blessing. I never did find out what else had happened under sedation. But I haven't seen Carmen since.

MISERABLE COW

'Where the bugger are we?' Karen asked despairingly. We'd been driving in the pitch black since leaving the motorway half hour before and hadn't seen a solitary street sign. That afternoon, I'd been given directions for this show the old fashioned way over the phone; this was in the days before the convenience of sat-nav. But what sounded quite pretty and picturesque was actually a nightmare in the dark. The road was full of potholes and we had to shout over the sound of the rain hammering the roof of the car. The motorway turn-off had been correct, but we couldn't be sure we'd gone the right way since.

Karen was a neighbour of mine and was driving me to the show. It was a Ladies Night, and she'd made no secret she'd only come to see the male strippers. 'Something big and black with a long tongue,' was how she'd described her requirements on the journey. I was already wishing I hadn't invited her. And to top it all, we now appeared to be lost. She was getting grumpy and I was getting equally vexed.

'There's a man over there, look,' she said. 'You can ask him directions. Go on, get out.'

'I'm not getting out here in the pitch black and pouring rain. We're in the middle of fuckin' nowhere. For all I know he could be an axe murderer or something!'

'Just ask him!' she screamed, 'We could be going in circles for hours and I'll miss the strippers.' I stepped cautiously from the car into a puddle that was deeper than my shoe. My eyes adjusted to the darkness and I could now see that the man was standing in a field next to a tall hedge. Why would he be there? I called 'hello?' to no answer. Shining my torch on his face I got a shock. It wasn't a man at all. It was a huge cow. It mooed with such ferocity that the car windows rattled. I returned a little rattled myself, filling my other shoe with water from the same puddle on the way back in.

'Is that a balloon on that gate post?' said Karen pointing. It looked more like a used condom flapping about in the rain, but it was the best clue so far that we may be in the right place. We drove up through the gate. A mere hundred yards ahead was what looked like a giant scout hut. Music was banging, lights were flashing, and we could see through the open entrance about two hundred women singing and dancing and milling about. We looked at each other in amazement. Where had all these women come from? Not thirty seconds before, we had appeared so far off the beaten track that we might as well have been on the moon.

The show itself was OK, though everything was running behind. We'd arrived so late that most of the audience were already too pissed to be of much use. Most of my night's work consisted of crowd control. I even asked at one point if there was a cattle prod I could borrow. Both the male strippers had the same trouble finding the place as we did. I was glad when it was all over.

By the time Karen and I came out the dressing room the place was already deserted. 'The sooner we're away from this bloody dump the better,' she said, sulking because she'd not pulled a stripper. Outside, the rain had finally stopped. Still pitch dark there was just an eerie silence, interrupted only by the distance sound of a group of women laughing. They had all dispersed from the scout hut like ants disappearing back into the undergrowth and across the fields, not another car in sight.

Climbing back into ours, I took a deep sigh. Karen started the engine, but when she tried to pull away, nothing happened. 'Oh no, you're not stuck in the mud are you? Not after the night we've already had!' We climbed back out to have a look. Everything seemed to be in order at the rear. But lying across the front of the car was that huge cow from earlier. It had settled down to sleep, I suppose across the front of what had been a warm engine. We couldn't back out because of a fence. And the cow was adamant that it was there for the night. We pushed it and shoved it. Tried to entice it out of the way with grass. Even Rowntree's Fruit Pastilles didn't work. It responded by wrapping it's fourteen-inch tongue around a screaming Karen's ankle, the closest she'd come to her original requirements for the night. She whinged and moaned non-stop whilst trying to remove cow saliva from her tights by pouring Evian over it and shaking her leg. I'm not sure which of the two was the bigger cow or the more miserable. I longed once more for the cattle prod.

REALITY GADGET

As you probably realise by now, I'm never one to gossip. But a few years back, there was one discreet little titbit that I just couldn't keep to myself. I was pregnant. Yes! It may have come as a bit of a surprise to some of you. Probably not quite as much as it was to my partner Charlie, who upon hearing promptly dived head first into a bottle of Bailey's Irish Cream. At the time, the only pitter-patter of tiny feet in our lives was that of our two adorable Persian pussies Chelsea and Lucy. But I was nesting like a woman possessed. I even put a baby mobile over the top of Chelsea's basket, much to her disgust. She took one look at it and pounced, hissing and spitting like an old dear at a jumble sale. Being quite an elderly lady herself, she then had to lie down for half an hour before tumbling the colour coordinated baby rattle down three flights of stairs and promptly out of the window onto Old Compton Street.

The reality of course, was that Chelsea need not have felt threatened by a pending new arrival. I'd been trying out a gadget designed to enable expectant fathers to experience pregnancy for themselves, for a magazine article survey. It was like a hold-all full of house bricks, the sort of thing the military wear on their back to go jogging. The only difference was that it was on the front, tits and all. It's supposed to make men more sympathetic to a woman's difficulty in coping with the physical demands of carrying an unborn sprog. Closer to the truth, it was probably designed by a woman to make her man take a turn at the washing and ironing.

It was in the queue at the Post Office that I first realised I should have gone for a three-month rather than a nine-month gadget. My feet were throbbing and my back was aching. To make matters worse, it was Monday... pension day. The smell of stale piss from my companions in the queue was making me feel nauseous. At least I think it was the smell and not some kind of psychosomatic morning sickness. Bedraggled and unshaven, having slept in my gadget overnight, a lighter moment came when a miniature silver-haired darling offered me a Murray Mint and asked me, 'How long have you got to go, dear?' But no bastard offered me a seat on the bus during the journey back. By the time I reached home, I was ready to jack in the whole experience and throw the bloody thing out of the same window as the rattle. But of course, the whole point of the exercise is the experience itself, and I've never been a quitter.

My darling Charlie had cleaned up the apartment and cooked the dinner, which was a delight. But then he always does these things, so not much of a favour. So after eating I sent him out in the torrential rain to buy me things to satisfy my pregnant cravings. I had decided they were going to be After Dinner Mints and Cream Soda. These are each sold in separate shops, one at each end of Soho so quite a trial for him. But my logic was that if I was going to suffer carrying his fuckin' baby, he would have to suffer too. Still, Charlie being true to his nature didn't complain one little bit, so as he dried himself off with a towel my guilt began to set in. Perhaps I was being too literal about this experience. It was after all my idea and I hadn't asked him to join in. His support was purely out of love. Feeling a little awkward, I reached for a cigarette. They weren't there. I winched myself up out of the chair and wandered around trying to remember where I had put them down. Is forgetfulness a symptom of advanced pregnancy? Or just the onset of Alzheimer's?

'What you looking for, babe?' asked Charlie, lovingly.

'Where are my fags?' I asked. He reached forward and held my hand sympathetically.

'Look, if you're going to take this seriously my angel, cravings and all, then you've got to go all the way. So I flushed them down the toilet.' In an instant, my guilt evaporated and became steam from my ears. Revenge is sweet, even if it's someone else's.

So what did I learn from the experience of my pregnancy gadget? A new level in back pain? A deeper respect for expectant mothers? That Charlie gives as good as he gets? My biggest impression actually came as quite a surprise to me. Lying in bed wearing my gadget for the last night, I had a brief magical moment where I suddenly believed that this experience would end with the birth of our own child. Then of course sadly, reality returned.

HUMUNGOUS DERRIERE

The only reason I'd agreed to do it was to see for myself just how big that arse really was. Meet n' greet had never really been my thing, although a clever idea... a group of fabulously sparkling professional extroverts to welcome you at the entrance of a club, making it look as though your time inside would be just that bit more special than in reality. Perfect job for a dolled up drag queen, especially on a night like this when we were expecting such a whopping pair of buttocks to grace our presence. Yes, Jennifer Lopez was due along with an entourage of about fifty clingers-on. They'd cleared the whole VIP area for the purpose, though we'd already placed our bets that it'd be a no-show. Vince the doorman was adamant she drank out in Romford all the time. Personally, I just think he was desperate to believe his own life was more glamorous. Karen on the pay desk had a glittery shoe on her back shelf that she swore blind Dannii Minogue had once left behind. Despite it being perhaps easier to imagine Dannii eating a kebab on a Saturday night out in Essex than J-Lo, I wasn't convinced she would have got back down two flights of concrete stairs from the VIP Lounge and back in her limo without noticing her shoe was missing, even after four bottles of Lambrini, two Babyshams and a pickled egg.

I had seen Jennifer Lopez's arse before. Well, in theory I had. It was actually at Madame Tussaud's. Rumour had it they'd had to melt down several lesser members of the royal family to have enough wax. Though I have to confess, I didn't get that good a look because I was a little distracted. A rather beamy woman in a pink shell-suit was having her picture taken with George Clooney when his arm came off in her hand. After several minutes of rather hysterical screaming she went into an asthma attack and fell gasping to the floor. One of the teenage tour guides tried desperately to detach her vice-like grip from Mr Clooney's leg before his trousers also came off. The stupid youth hit the woman on the fingers with his torch. She did let go, but only to punch him in the face. As the crowd parted, he flew backwards and landed under a table at the feet of Jonathan Ross. The woman's face was already quite blue by the time the paramedic had untangled his knapsack from Shirley Bassey's feather boa... he'd got it caught while pushing through the crowd. By this time, J-Lo's arse had shrunk to comparative insignificance.

'They've had this red carpet steam-washed especially for tonight,' said Maureen, one of my co-meet n' greeters.

'I hope they've got it dry in time,' I said. 'Otherwise, by the time she's dragged that humungous derriere across it, it'll be all wet like she's pissed herself.' I couldn't understand why Maureen was dressed as a budgie. She said that her agent had phoned her about the job while she was on a noisy train. She had misheard "Jenny from the block" as "any from Hitchcock" and at such short notice a budgie costume was the closest she could get to his film The Birds.

I myself was dressed to thrill in a full-length pink sequinned gown with matching gloves. It had a flared skirt, which had already been trodden on about eight times by the pedantic queen in the sky-blue two-piece with matching guest list clipboard. Every acid glance in my direction underlined a terror of being upstaged by the drag queen. Treading on my gown was on purpose and really getting on my wick. I was just about to punch his lights out when a black stretch limo pulled into the kerb. He nudged me backwards with his shoulder. As I fell into a tower of decorative foliage to the side of the entrance, he skipped forward and pulled open the limo door. He was of course expecting Jennifer Lopez herself to step elegantly from the car. But to my delight the limo wasn't full of glitzy entourage but rather a pissed-up group of Essex girls on a hen night. One leaned out of the car, grabbed the front of his jacket and threw up down his bespoke trousers. I laughed so much that one of my eyelashes fell off. Needless to say, J-Lo didn't show. But most of the people at the club that night had bought her new CD in anticipation. Makes you wonder how many clubs up and down the UK had been told she would be there on the night of her CD launch. So I didn't get to meet J-Lo after all. Still, could be worse... at least I wasn't covered in Essex girl sick!

SQUATTING IN THE KERB

I was driving through Billericay back to London from a cabaret performance when my eyes befell a scary sight. It was about 2am and, although late at night, the road was fairly well lit. I stopped behind a car sitting at a junction before us. Behind it in the middle of the road, my headlamps illuminated a rather dumpy woman squatting having a piss. She had long blonde hair, a sequinned boob tube and a short red leather skirt. As I approached, she looked up at me with an "I've started so I'll finish" kinda look, and then stuck two fingers up. When she'd finally emptied her bladder onto the public highway, she defiantly banged her hand on my bonnet shouting "Wanker!" then climbed back into her car. She drove forward three feet into the path of the crossing traffic and then stopped again, running back around to collect her forgotten Primark knickers from the back bumper.

Now, call me old fashioned, but women never used to behave like this! We've all had a piddle outside at one time or another. There used to be a coach take us all to the seaside for the day which would stop now and again for everyone to pee modestly in the relative privacy of the roadside flora... men one side, women the other. But with crouching in the middle of the road comes a new breed of woman.

Of course, I blame designer drinks. Where I come from, there was a time when the men would sup in the Saloon Bar while the ladies would delicately sip a gin and tonic or something equally appropriate in The Snug next door. They'd all have a sing-song, get drunk and stumble home, yet still attempt to appear relatively elegant. But with the arrival of Alcopops, the aim for some women became to get visibly as tanked up as possible, have a fight, stuff a kebab down their screech, throw up over the potential shag and then... evidently, squat in the kerb.

Don't get me wrong. I don't consider myself prudish. Having lived in Soho for a few years, even the really weird stuff doesn't seem that unusual. And I'm certainly not against the sale of Alcopops. When I had my little pub, it got through a dozen glorious cases a week. The brightly coloured bottles looked pretty in the backlit fridges and the profit from their sale had refurbished my jewellery case on more than one occasion. And may the baby Jesus be my witness, I don't really even have a gripe about some women draping their curtains on the tarmac to empty their bladder. No, indeed the problem lies much deeper. In fact, it touches the very soul.

I was watching a performance of Eartha Kitt on DVD the other day. There she was; a vision of style, sewn into a skin-tight, sequinned leopard patterned gown. With that dulcet, velvet voice of hers she was singing Under The Bridges Of Paris With You. Gentle and sexy. An elegant woman of the world, naughty but with panache. And believable. You knew the chances were she really had made love under a Parisian arch or two in her time. Deliciously decadent! Yet try as I may, I just can't picture her squatting behind a mate's

Fiat Uno for a slash. A man would need to fork out for Champagne and caviar in a five-grand-per-night hotel suite to catch a glimpse of our Eartha's clunge, not merely drive up the high street at two in the morning to the junction opposite Morrisons.

Eartha, Dusty, Judy, Barbra… and every old dame that's ever draped her pearls in a Babysham at the end of any bar from Soho's magical past. All are icons of certain elegance. Role models that have shaped the look and manner of every drag queen since cabaret began. We professionally emulate these role models whilst simultaneously adding a hint of trademark masculinity and crudity as a fourth dimension. It's ironic and it's our strength. So no, it wasn't getting a front seat view of the Billericay Flaps that was scary. It was this: now that some women are themselves adopting our testosterone-soaked mannerisms, the irony of drag queens is weakening. So you see ladies… every time you squat in the kerb, drag takes a step closer to the grave!

ATCHOO... THANK YOU!

I was feeling a bit bunged up. Yes, I'm afraid to say it was the dreaded flu. But not just any old flu, oh no. It wasn't even man flu... it was much worse than that. It was drag queen flu. Though in fairness it is similar to man flu only with a lot more drama. As my partner Charlie put it, when I've got flu, I deserve an Oscar and a standing ovation. "Atchoo... thank you, thank you..." Of course, in my opinion he was talking rubbish. OK so I did throw my dinner plate up the wall, but anyone would after six hours watching Countdown huddled up in bed with nothing but a hot water bottle to cuddle.

'I need consoling,' I cried.

'Console yourself, I'm busy!' he replied selfishly. The least he could have done for me was a bed bath. And a more caring well-wisher had sent me a huge bunch of grapes that still needed hand-feeding. I thought for a moment. How does one console oneself without a giant box of Dairy Milk? And more importantly, what's the point of all that suffering if there's nobody there to see you do it? At least Judy Garland had an audience. My diva status was being deprived. I decided to get up and spread my germs around Soho. I was after all a very giving person.

Charlie had evidently put the word around. Everyone I knew was giving me a very wide berth, just when I needed sympathy and a hug. I dropped to my knees in the middle of Old Compton Street and screamed, 'I've got a cold, not bloody Leprosy!'

'Are you making a film?' asked a passing lady, glancing around for the camera.

'No I'm not, I've just got the worse flu in the history of Soho and nobody cares,' I complained.

'Ahh… would you like an Opal Fruit?' Through tears I declined graciously and headed on up the street.

'Big Issue, sir?' asked one friendly street vendor.

'Big issue? Big issue?! I'll tell ya what the big issue is here… today… right now. No one gives a damn. I'm miserable and in pain, with a blinding headache, streaming eyes and a runny nose. I'm aching in places I didn't even know I had and I'm probably at this moment in time very close to death. Shall I tell you what the big issue of the day is? Everyone has deserted me just when I need them most, and quite frankly I may as well go jump off Westminster Bridge for all anyone cares. Big issue? Yes, it bloody well is!' Looking a little shocked, he offered me a pound coin.

'You look as though you need this more than I do,' he said. Rather taken aback by my own outburst, I bought one of his magazines and headed off to the Co-op. Comfort food was what I needed.

When I was a youngster, I was addicted to Dairylea cheese spread. In fact, my Mother still has a candid photo of me, in our kitchen at home with half a dozen slices of bread smeared with my favourite comfort food lined up on the worktop. I wandered around the Co-op for ten minutes and still couldn't find any. A young man approached timidly and touched my arm.

'I'm sorry, but I heard you mumbling to yourself and you seem distressed. Are you looking for Jesus?' I couldn't believe my ears. A Jehovah's Witness touting for business is one thing, but at the Co-op? I was riled.

'Look, each to their own but I think you're out of order bringing this sort of thing here,' I ranted uncontrollably, practically foaming at the mouth. 'I'm just minding my own business doing a bit of harmless shopping and you want to ram your religion down my throat as though suddenly it's going to solve all my problems and cure my flu in the blink of an eye? Well I'm sorry, but there's a time and a place for everything and I truly wish you everything you wish for yourself, but if I ever feel the need to find Jesus, I'll find him for myself, in Church, without anyone else's encouragement or persuasion. Are you understanding me? Are you getting what I'm saying?!' The poor young man looked mortified.

'Erm…' he stuttered. 'I said "cheeses", not Jesus. Are you looking for cheeses? Only, I thought I heard you mutter Dairylea? Well… it's in aisle three.' With that he turned and scurried away like a little spooked dormouse. A group of fellow shoppers had stopped what they were doing to listen. Now they were shaking their heads in disgust. I wanted to die! Clearly my ears were a bit bunged up too. I left my basket on a big pile of prawns and fled the store.

'I told you not to go out in that state,' said Charlie, passing me another tissue. He was of course right.

'Whenever you get the flu, you're like Mother Bear with a sore head.' It was true. 'You get yourself all distressed because life goes on around you and you feel neglected and deprived.' He wasn't wrong. 'And besides, you can be such a bitch!' Hold on a minute... well, fair comment I suppose.

'Yeah, I know,' I said remorsefully.

'Anyway,' he smiled, 'I'd already been to the Supermarket and got you this.' He handed me a plate of Dairylea on toast. 'And when you've finished your main course, here's your pudding,' he said, pulling back the bed quilt to reveal the biggest box of Dairy Milk I'd ever seen. I was choked, if not a little embarrassed by all the fuss I'd made. So now there I was, propped up in bed surrounded by tissues, chocolates and toast like some caricature from Carry On Nurse, watching yet more episodes of the blessed Countdown and counting my blessings for Charlie and his wisdom. Feeling like hell, humbled by my actions of the day and praying to "cheeses" that everyone I'd upset could forgive me, just one simple question occupied my mind. Where the bugger was Carol Vorderman?

AZURE BLUE

Why did life have to be so complicated? What a week I'd had. Everything was stressful and nothing straight forward. And to top it all, I'd had a call to say that my Aunt was in hospital, though nothing too scary thankfully. I'd been told she was at King's College in London. At the time, I was living above and running a pub as well as my cabaret show, so I didn't have a lot of free time. Going to visit her in hospital would need planning. With this in mind, I'd allowed myself twenty minutes to get there in a taxi.

'Which King's d'ya want then?' said the Cabbie.

'I only know about the one in Chelsea!' I replied.

'No, they're all over the place mate... you'd better check.' It turned out to be the one in Camberwell... forty minutes away through the rush hour... more unanticipated stress and complications. I finally arrived at the very end of visiting hours, though to be fair the fabulous nurses didn't rush me. Still, I'd been advised to get a bus back. Thankfully there was one that ran door-to-door.

Now take this as you may, but I hadn't been on a bus for about twenty years, so it was somewhat of a novelty for me. And thirty pounds cheaper than a cab, though seeing my Aunt was of course priceless.

Taking my seat on the empty upper deck, I tried to remember the last time I had been on a bus...

It had been a beautiful day and I was once again upstairs, though it was open-topped. The sun was warm, and the breeze was blowing through my hair (yes, it really was that long ago). Every so often, the sunlight was dappled as we passed under a roadside tree, each one shaped over time by the constant flow of buses through the leaves. But the thing that'd stuck in my mind was the old woman a few seats in front of me. She was very fidgety and kept standing up. Unfortunately, someone had thrown a pair of boots into the branches of a tree ahead. They were dangling by the laces and kicked her smack in the centre of the forehead as we passed under. Her false teeth landed in the lap of the young girl in the seat behind, who screamed and promptly threw them over the side of the bus. They landed on the road where they were then run over by a tarmac lorry. There was a great kerfuffle as the bus was stopped and her smile retrieved. Miraculously, they had not broken. But I remember the bus conductor handing them back to her and, I suppose in shock, she put them straight back into her mouth without so much as blowing the dirt off.

'Would you call that azure blue or not?' I was startled from my daydream.

'What... what, sorry are you speaking to me?'

'Azure blue? Is that azure blue or not? Oh, I can't see it properly under these lights without my glasses.' A little old lady had appeared from nowhere and sat on the seat in front of me. I think the biggest shock was her uncanny resemblance to the toothless woman in my daydream. From a plastic Marks and Spencer bag, she dangled a brightly coloured cardigan sleeve over the back of the seat in my direction.

'I... err... why do you need your glasses to see what colour it is?' I mused.

'You've got a point,' she replied. With a disgruntled sigh, she threw it back into the bag and screwed it shut. 'Well, she can do 'er own shopping from now on, I'm right peeved with it I am. Peeved. If she's gonna be so fussy, why don't she just do it herself? Don't misread me, I do like blue. But what's to know if it's turquoise or azure blue? And what about that aquamarine? Well, I don't know, really I don't.'

I was a bit lost for words. 'Friend of yours, is she?'

'Aw no, she's not no friend of mine. Not anymore, least ways. The old lush. No she's like her in that film... oh, what's it called? The Ginger Dwarf...'

'Err... The Wizard of Oz?' I offered.

'No, not Judy Garland... Elizabeth Taylor.'

'Elizabeth Taylor? Ginger Dwarf?'

'Yes. Supposed to be frightening, but I wasn't afraid. There weren't even a dwarf in it.' She was baffling.

'You don't mean Who's Afraid of Virginia Wolf, do you?' I couldn't help but grin.

'Yes that's it, just like that she is. Filthy tart. She can do her own bleeding shopping from now on. I went up Marksie's special, but she won't like it I know she won't. "Get me a new bra and some drawers," she told me. So I turns round and I says to her, 'what do you want with drawers, waste of money that'd be on you! I won't be doing it again. It's all so… complicated!' she said, screwing her brow.

And there was me thinking my life was complicated. In reality it's simply a matter of degree. One woman's stress is another's distraction.

CANTEEN CHICKEN

I'd spent four days researching every Irene Handl film I could find. Once a film in which you have a role is released to the world it's out there forever, and though this was only a small part, it was still important to get it right. After all, Dame Judy had won an Oscar for just eight minutes on screen in Shakespeare In Love. I'd been told I was to play a canteen char lady in a mechanics' garage and that I had to bring my own costume and do my own makeup. Though a late-night shoot, I arrived at the studio early to give myself time to prepare and get into character.

I lightened my complexion to age myself. I had a flowery wrap-around pinafore with a little padding to make me stout, a brown turban with a grey wig and a cheap nineteen-sixties broach by way of a hint of my character's desire for glamour in her dull life. I even added a facial mole for effect.

As I walked onto the set, everyone ignored me. I approached the director.

'This is a closed set love, you'll have to come back tomorrow if you want to clean,' he said complacently.

'No I'm Jeff Kristian... the drag queen... for the canteen scene?' He looked me up and down impatiently.

'No, no that's not the look at all! We want you to be the busty blonde tart like your publicity photo.' That's nice, I thought! 'How's our mechanic Zeus going to flirt with you dressed like that? Get changed... and quickly!' Bugger! Zeus? That's a funny name for a mechanic. Perhaps it was a Greek character.

Anyway, luckily I had other costumes in the boot of my car. On went the red sequins, the dumb blonde wig, heaps of makeup and jewellery and the biggest pair of tits I could find... I even rolled up a few spare pairs of tights to poke behind them for dramatic effect. The Director was delighted.

'OK, now there's just one line.' He shoved a sheet of paper under my nose and walked away. It said, "Picks up teapot and says, 'do you want it hot and sweet?' Then chicken on counter." So far so good. Though the teapot was empty and there wasn't any chicken in sight. So while I was waiting, I made myself useful and popped into one of the side rooms off set to fill the pot with hot tea to add reality to my role.

By the time I'd got back the Director was flapping. 'Where have you been? Come on, Zeus is ready. Now... hold the teapot aloft... he enters... you flirt and say your line.'

'There's no cups,' I observed. 'Shouldn't there be cups?'

'No, they'll just get in the way. OK. Silence studio... and action!' I held the teapot aloft. In walked Zeus. But he wasn't the short fat motor-oil covered character actor I was expecting. He was about six foot four, heavily tanned and head to foot in muscles tattoos and piercings... and completely naked with an erection like a hearth log. It was then I realised... I was in a porn film! In shock I dropped the teapot, which smashed on the counter, spraying hot tea in all directions including Zeus' naked body. He cried out in pain.

'Cut! Cut! Cut!' screamed the Director. 'What the fuck are you doing?' he yelled at me.

'I'm so sorry, I was just a bit surprised when Zeus came out. He wasn't what I was expecting!'

'What were you expecting?'

'Well… a short fat Greek.' He looked at me dumbfounded. 'Where did the tea come from? It's a prop, not a real teapot!' And there were no real tea towels to dry Zeus down. I did the best I could with my compact powder pad while someone scouted the building for something to clear up the mess. Zeus seemed to quite enjoy it, though my hands were shaking like Dorothy's pigtails in the tornado by the time I'd finished. There wasn't another teapot, so I had to offer him a mug instead.

'And… action!'

'Do you want it hot and sweet?'

'Every time!' came Zeus' reply, as he grabbed a young blonde guy from one side and ripped off his green overalls to reveal that he too was naked. I hadn't even noticed him standing there, what with all the earlier drama and that hearth log resting on the front of my counter. Zeus picked him up and threw him onto the pale blue Formica surface in front of me. I understood now why the cups would be in the way. And "chicken" was clearly a reference to this young stud, not the roast dinner with baked potatoes and Brussels sprouts that I'd anticipated as a prop from my canteen. He lay there for a moment looking up at me, with all his fit young bits pointing proudly into the air. I couldn't think where to put my face! But thankfully by this time, they'd decided the canteen lady had been a bad idea and that I could get my fee and go home.

Several weeks later I saw an eccentric elderly man walking down Old Compton Street. Not particularly memorable, other than the fact that he had a chicken on his head. I thought of Zeus…

CLOSET OF DESIRE

I'm not one for parties really. I'd usually just rather sit in front of the telly with a mug of Cup-a-Soup and file me toenails. But Romie's famous annual do was on the way home from my performance as Cliff Richard in Colchester. And as usual it was fancy dress, so I could just keep my costume on and come as The Young One himself. The reason Romie's was always so successful is because the guests were all people you really should stay in touch with but really didn't want to, so a party once a year was perfect. It was just enough to catch up on who'd been screwing who, who'd had what done to which part of their body, who'd been in rehab... basically get all the gossip and exit before anyone had had a chance to find out anything too derogatory about you.

Upon arrival, I had a lot of trouble trying to park. That's often the problem with fancy dress; everyone comes by car because nobody wants to be seen as Elvis on the bus. Well, not in the suburbs anyway. When I lived in Soho, people wandered around dressed in crazy outfits all the time, which can be surprisingly useful. Particularly for someone like me who can't always be arsed to whip out the Gaultier just to pop to the corner shop. Rather, just tell everyone you're in fancy dress and blame the celebrity you look most like. There's many a time I've picked up twenty Silk Cut and a pint of semi-skimmed dressed as Britney during her breakdown.

Having finally found a parking space, I tapped on the front door but nobody could hear me over the loud music. I banged harder and a woman opened the door claiming to be dressed as Sharon Osbourne, though she looked to me more like Olive from On The Buses.

'Oh my God, you've come as Mike Reid!' she exclaimed, teaching me to keep my mouth shut. By this time, I was busting for a piddle.

'Where's the loo, Sharon?' I asked Olive.

'The Closet Of Desire is upstairs on the right babe,' she answered.

'Closet Of Desire? Why's it called that?'

''Cause it's where ya go when ya desire a dump.' Ask a silly question!

Turning the light on in the loo was a bit of a shock. The entire room had been done head to toe in mirror mosaic. Even the ceiling, the floor and the back of the door were covered in it. This was gonna be like having a piss inside a mirror ball. In the corner, a lava lamp lit up the room in such a way as to make it feel like you were underwater. I stood for a while unable to generate any flow, despite a full bladder. I'm not sure what was putting me off more; the sea-sickness or the fact that everywhere I looked I could see Cliff Richard with his knob out. In the end I had shut my eyes. I don't think I missed the bowl… it was hard to tell underwater. It took me a while to find the sink, which was also mirrored. But that was nothing compared to finding the door handle. Try as I may, I just couldn't find a way out. I shouted for help a few times but, as before, could not be heard over the music. I even banged on the door, but the mirror pieces were quite sharp to the touch.

After twenty minutes, I'd had enough and decided to climb out of the window. Outside just below my floor level there was a concrete ledge above the front door, if I could just manage to get a footing without tearing my costume. It took a bit of athletic manoeuvring, but Cliff was finally out of the closet.

However, I wasn't really that much better off. It was now raining and, short of plummeting two meters into the roses either side of the concrete path, I was stuck. I don't know how long I was up there, but after what seemed like an hour, a cagouled man with a small constantly yapping dog spied me as he walked past. It didn't stop him though, he carried on walking and, like a fool, I was too embarrassed to call out to him. Ten minutes later he returned, no doubt on his way back home.

'You alright, mate?' he called up to me.

'I can't get down,' I replied. 'Can you get some help, please?' He rubbed his chin. Then he and the dog looked at each other.

'I could knock the door I suppose, Rolie?' I'm standing on a death ledge at two in the morning in suburbia, dripping wet and dressed as Cliff Richard and he's asking the dog what to do?

'No, don't knock...' If Olive found out, I'd never hear the end of it. 'Just push that wheelie bin over, it'll break my fall.' Thankfully he did.

'My wife's a big fan,' he gushed. 'Wait till I tell her I helped Mike Reid down off someone's roof with a wheelie bin. She'll be chuffed to bits!' I didn't say anything.

THE KIRBY GRIP OF DOOM

I can remember some years ago running out into the front garden like every other neighbour down our street, to see why there was a police car and ambulance outside old Mrs Dunwoody's house at number fourteen. She was a nice enough woman, though a bit of a busybody in her time. But still quite useful in her way. "If you want anything to get around, just tell Mrs Dunwoody and the whole street will know within the hour," they'd say. So we did. And we did. But the irony to this story is that we never did truly find out anything about her own demise because there was no longer a Mrs Dunwoody to knock and tell us.

Rumour had it that she'd committed suicide by putting her left foot in a washing up bowl of water while poking a Kirby grip into a plug socket. Apparently, while writhing about in spasms of shock, she'd knocked over a pot plant. Knowing what a clean freak she was, I think it more likely she'd knocked the plant over first and was clearing it up, using the Kirby grip to get the soil out of the hole.

But what a sad thing to think anyone could be so unhappy that they'd want to end their life earlier than nature had intended. I recall someone from our local supermarket jumping into the Thames. Mind you to be fair, it was Budgen's. But bless her heart, being a pearl short of a twin-set she jumped at low tide and they had to call the River Police to prise her out of the mud. But then she threatened to sue them because they tore her jacket in the process... odd considering she didn't seem to mind it floating up the river on a corpse. Perhaps an indication that she wasn't in her right mind at the time, as I suspect is the case with many other poor souls in the same boat... or mud.

I was once asked to man a gay Samaritans-type phone line as a drag queen for two hours every Monday night after Eastenders. The brief was that suicides might be avoided if we could "cheer them up a bit". I'm not sure how relevant the Eastenders aspect was. But then some of the storylines are so depressing that perhaps you'd want to jump under a bus after watching. But I honestly couldn't bring myself to do it. It's one thing trying to bring on a smile on stage a couple of times a week but trying to talk some poor bastard down off a rooftop with jokes about Mary Poppins is a different ball of wax altogether.

But I did once get three points on my license driving across London at break-neck speed while on the mobile. I was trying to keep someone talking and awake after an overdose. I was somewhat relieved upon arrival to discover that he was so drunk he'd swallowed a whole jar of Vitamin E tablets by mistake. I remember thinking at the time, he may be depressed but he'll have fabulous skin-tone. He explained through lots of tears and some considerable snot that it was a middle-aged-mother-gay-son thing and all quite sad. He'd been trying to explain that being gay was probably genetic, and she was convinced it was something from his childhood. Apparently, knitting had made him a Homosexual. I suggested perhaps if I got some wool he'd make one for me too, but he couldn't see the funny side.

I think it's a brave person who contemplates ending it all. I couldn't do it, no matter how bad things appeared to be. And I'm not sure how I'd do it if I wanted to. I could leap from the top of my own stiletto shoes I suppose. My partner Charlie's occasionally suggested I try eating my own cooking. And I've died on stage quite a few times, though perhaps that doesn't count. But I did get knocked over a wall dressed as Diana Ross once when a car mounted the pavement in Trafalgar Square, though that was more attempted murder than a bid for suicide. Well, it felt like attempted murder at the time. Some people just don't like Diana Ross, I guess.

My philosophy is this. If you ever find you've had enough of your own life, just steal someone else's! Never underestimate how much fun Celebrity Stalking can be. Though it can be expensive, so maybe not the best solution if your problem is money. Or you could just donate yourself to someone else. There're plenty of slave dungeons in Amsterdam looking for contributions. But if nothing else will do, remember this… when you jam that Kirby grip into a plug socket, you could be depriving a drag queen somewhere of a hair do.

TWILIGHT TITS

'She's about the same size as me,' I said nervously. The shop assistant squinted suspiciously. It wasn't easy to ask for what I needed in a shop when I first began drag as a profession. Nowadays, pretty much anything that could possibly be required for a show can be acquired with a quick scout on the internet and a credit card. But back in the days before computers when we only had black and white telly (well perhaps not quite that far back), finding a suitable item over the counter was not so easy… especially when it came to corsetry.

'I see,' replied the girl knowingly. My palms were sweating. Then she winked. Or at least I think it was a wink and not some kind of twitch or lazy eye. But the possibility that it could be a wink made things even tenser. Now the very bollocks that were in question also began to sweat and I wanted the floor to open, allowing me to plunge back into unquestioned obscurity.

Getting the size right was the real problem. As archaic as it may seem, a geezer just can't walk into C&A and try on a frock. It's got nothing to do with sweaty armpits or splitting seams, it's purely because a given shop can't be seen by Middle England to be supporting the possibility of Transvestism and all the filthy, perverse related activities… like abducting children, Nazism, murdering old ladies and the like. As time went on, I had a much clearer knowledge of what to look for. But back at the beginning it was all still a mystery and rather embarrassing.

'Perhaps you can take it home and, erm, let "her" try it on. Then if it doesn't fit, you can always bring it back with the receipt and change it,' the shop assistant said, making an effort to be helpful. I took a deep breath and leapt from the precipice.

'Actually it's for me,' I said, cautiously. 'I'm a professional drag queen and I need it for my show.' The relief on her face was staggering. She actually started breathing for the first time in ten minutes.

'Ah, so "she" is your alter ego?' We were reduced to whispering now. In reality, it had far more to do with paying the rent than ego, but at least suddenly she was my new Stylist. 'Follow me,' she said, now on a mission. We sped through to the relative safety of the Gents department. Grabbing a random pair of trousers as a raison d'etre, she took me by the hand and led me to a fitting cubicle.

'I've brought you in here to measure you up,' she whispered excitedly, pulling a concealed tape measure from her substantial cleavage. 'You're a size twelve, my darling.' Coming out to her had apparently enabled us to now use terms of endearment towards each other. She threw back the cubicle curtain to reveal a little group of her colleagues crouched together listening, no doubt assuming there was something sexual and sinister going on. 'It's alright, he's a drag queen!' she explained with glee.

'Oh!' came the relieved group response... now it all made sense! I wasn't a conquest, I was just a special secret little project. But suddenly the whole store became my oyster. I had about six of them, bringing me everything from chiffon evening dresses to diamante earrings. They were even arguing amongst themselves as to what would make me too "tarty" or "frumpy." In fifteen minutes I'd gone from being that embarrassing gentleman to the star novelty attraction. More surreally, they were all winking at me simultaneously now, as though something in the canteen tea had infected them all with a nervous nadger. It was like The Twilight Zone… with tits!

I decided to just agree to buy everything they offered me and sort it all out when I got home. The sooner this was over the better and I was in no hurry to undergo this type of excruciating torture again any time soon. With about fifteen shopping bags, I made my way to the exit. A little party of well-wishing shop assistants had gathered by the doors to see me off with smiles and waves. A few of the other customers had also stopped to bid me farewell… someone even took a photo! They'd clearly noticed all the fuss and perhaps believed I may be some kind of local celebrity. I suppose in a small reality, perhaps now I was.

I sat at home wondering how bored they must all have been for me to be such an excitement. And I was starving hungry… I hadn't been able to buy food as planned. Aside from not being able to carry any additional bags, I'd spent so much money panic buying that I didn't have any left. Much more of this and I'd be down to a size eight. Then none of my new costumes would fit me anyway.

THE GHOSTS OF MOLLY MOGGS

Yeah, yeah… let's get all the "put the willies up me" jokes out the way now. But the little drag pub I once ran in London's gay district really was haunted. Molly Moggs was built around 1732 and stood on the corner of Old Compton Street and Charing Cross Road, one of Soho's famous Grade Two listed buildings. She was a crooked little thing… my bathroom floor at the top had a nine-inch slope, which could be a bugger on the lino getting out the bath with wet feet. On more than one occasion I slid clean across the floor and landed in the sink. But despite all of this, Molly Moggs was a gem and it's quite easy to understand why someone would not want to leave when their time on Earth had come to an end. I may even consider haunting it myself!

As far as we were aware there were two ghosts. The scarier of the two resided mostly in the cellars. It was believed that this part of the building was considerably older. Charing Cross Road has only been so-called since 1880. An earlier name was Hog Lane. This was not a reference to Soho's inhabitants I'm pleased to say, but to the pig market that used to reside close to where Centrepoint now towers. Most of Soho would have been quite newly built upon what had been farmland, so you can begin to see the sort of people that used to hang around. It's believed there was an alley from the cellars out to Little Compton Street, more recently a service tunnel but still to this day visible down through the cattle grid in the middle of Charing Cross Road outside Molly's entrance. One can only imagine what kind of skulduggery this secret exit from the cellars was used for, but the ghost of the man from the cellar appeared to be from this Hog Lane period. He liked jumping out on people, which was not good for the nerves of more delicate staff or clientele. He first introduced himself to me and Charlie at four am one night as we slept, by jumping on the bed.

'What the bugger was that?' I shouted, to which the spirit replied quite loudly in a gruff voice, "Clive". Thankfully, he never spoke to us again.

The other ghost was a Victorian lady. A Lady in what sense we were unsure, being in Soho, but she was thankfully considerably friendlier than Clive. It was Charlie who first picked up the name Matilda. Soho has a history of mid nineteenth-century French settlers, arriving to escape the suppression of The Paris Commune, so the ghost's true name was more likely to be Mathilde. Complete with corset, bustle and bonnet, she loved to wear both the colour and scent of lavender. She adored the joie de vivre of Molly Moggs with its glitter and glamour and never-ending procession of weekly drag queens on stage. A Clairvoyant told us that aside from living there, she used to run the place and that she loved what we had done to keep it alive. And it was clear she had some business savvy. Knowing her opinion of us, I had on more than one occasion sat at my desk and asked for her help or advice. Usually, within ten minutes an answer arrived in the form of a letter, phone call or coincidence beyond what I'd have considered to be the norm. It's easy to be sceptical, but in business it's often wise to trust what works. And for me, Mathilde worked very well.

The other thing I admired about Mathilde was her attitude. She was a tough old bird, and she was quite happy to make her opinion known. This was particular when it came to the business of defending and protecting Molly Moggs. It was probably the smallest pub in Soho, and for this reason we had to have a strict customer policy which read, "Be Nice or Leave." To an offending party, one or two of the staff's stern words were occasionally followed by a smack from Mathilde, usually by way of a beer glass flying from the shelf and hitting them. The glass never broke, but the telling off was always heeded.

Perhaps the best example of this diva's repertoire was a warning. We sadly had to let a member of staff go for pilfering. Last thing one night after the bar had closed and all the cleaning up had been finished, a few of our more loyal remaining team members were standing at the end of our counter discussing the whole issue. They watched aghast as the staff tip jar, their bastion of freedom within Molly Moggs, rose from the back of the shelf, floated sideways across the room and dropped, smashing into a hundred pieces on the floor in front of the till.

I don't know whether or not the current owners are aware of our two ghosts, or any others. I'm just pleased they didn't follow us to our current home.

MAGICAL MYSTERY MARMITE

It's every woman's prerogative to be mysterious. Wherever and whenever I used to perform in my drag show, I would attempt to become the essence of mystique and drama. It wasn't always easy in six-inch heels, but I made the effort and I tried. Still as time trickled by, much of life had become routine. So a Magical Mystery Tour sounded like an opportunity not to be missed.

The ticket said ten a.m., which was a bit of a push for me being such a late riser. But if I wanted adventure I had to go out and get it, I'd decided. A week later I was standing in the freezing cold at a designated bus stop with about thirty elderly men and women, wondering what the bugger I'd let myself in for. Other than an ugly ginger brat who'd come with his grandma, I was the youngest one there. He kept staring at me. I tried to ignore him, but then he started to poke me in the back.

'What?'

'Oi, how old are you?' he asked sarcastically, sniffing a lump of hanging green snot back up his freckled nose.

'Thirty-nine, though I don't know what it's got to do with you.'

'You ain't thirty-nine. I reckon you're about fifty.' It was only out of respect for grandma that I didn't deck the little runt.

'I've not had much sleep,' I argued.

'I bet you tell everyone that!' he came back viciously.

I had by this time made up my mind to go home and go back to bed. But suddenly the coach arrived. Well, I say coach… more of a tin bucket on wheels, really. It screeched to a halt to a round of applause and much cooing from the old ladies. The door sprang open after a bit of a tug from the driver, and out stepped the tour guide dressed in a shocking pink satin Sergeant Pepper suit.

'Good morning ladies and gents and welcome to today's Magical Mystery Tour!'

'Yeah!' they all cheered collectively.

'Sounds like a pile of shite to me,' moaned Chucky. I was beginning to agree, though I thought him awfully rude.

'You shouldn't say things like that!' I scolded in the absence of his gran, who was having trouble getting her left leg up onto the bottom step.

'Aw, shut up! I'm ten years old, I'm a grown-up,' he scoffed. Hmm.

'Is this thing safe?' I asked the guide.

'Yeah, nothing to worry about mate. She's got another fifty years in her yet, more than I can say for some of these old biddies.' I didn't much like his attitude, either.

'Can I just ask, why are you dressed in a Sergeant Pepper costume?' I asked.

'I'm Paul McCartney… from the album? You know… The Magical Mystery Tour? The Beatles?'

'That wasn't Sergeant Pepper, that was a completely different album altogether,' I commented. I thought he was going to slap me. 'Shall I just get on?' I sheepishly climbed aboard.

I took the last remaining seat. To my horror, Chucky was just across the aisle. 'Who the fuck are The Beatles?' he asked. I ignored him.

'Hello there, my name's Violet,' said the old lady sitting next to me by the window.

'Hello dear, I'm Jeff. That's a pretty name... Violet,' I offered.

'D'ya think so? I hate it. I wish they'd called me Miranda or something. Still, we get what we come here with and leave with what's left I suppose.'

'Oh!' I was a little taken aback. 'Well... why didn't you just call yourself Miranda?'

'You know, I could have done couldn't I? Nobody would have known any different. They're all dead now anyway, I'm the only one left. Here, have a seedless grape!' She held out the bag to me.

'Yes I will. Thank you Miranda!' She smiled back with a mischievous twinkle in her eye. Everyone moaned at a loud feedback whistle as Paul turned on a microphone at the front.

'Well ladies and gents, are you all ready?'

'Yes!' came the excited reply.

'Today's Marvellous Magical Mystery Tour is so named after the song on The Sergeant Pepper Album by The Beatles...' he growled, looking in my direction, '... and is brought to you by Reliable Coach Tours Limited of Hackney. Today, we will be visiting... wait for it...' excitement was building. I could hardly contain myself by this time. 'A Marmite mine!'

'Hooray!' they all shouted.

'Ooh, how exciting,' said Miranda. 'I love Marmite I do. It's a funny thing you know, how you either love it or hate it. Do you like Marmite? We might be able to buy fresh a jar today when we're there.'

Chucky poked me again. 'Oi, are you a poofter?' I was gobsmacked.

'I beg your pardon?'

'Only that's what my Dad calls poofters, Marmite miners.' I suddenly realised that Paul's imaginary Marmite Mine was a reference to my being gay. Though upon reflection, I wasn't the one wearing the pink satin suit.

Reliable Coach Tours Limited of Hackney managed to get us to the next bus stop before smoke began billowing from under the bonnet. The tour was over before it had begun. Chucky began crying.

'Good job you're a grown-up,' I teased. And like the coach, Paul too looked a little broken. Still I couldn't resist revenge.

'It was Ringo who wore the pink, you know? Paul wore blue. I'll get my refund from the ticket office, shall I?' Steeped with glee I stepped off the coach and hailed a taxi.

MERM AS IN SPERM

Charlie and I settled down in front of our telly with a cup of cocoa and a finger to watch a new documentary about the then impending Royal Wedding of the gorgeous Kate Middleton to Prince William. Promising to be an in-depth insight into the special day, all we really got was a load of so-called experts telling us what might, perhaps just maybe happen. Being as keen as the rest of the nation to learn any little advanced titbit, we went to bed somewhat disappointed.

As I drifted into a deep sleep there was a sound of horse's hooves. Suddenly I was on the back of a large stallion with a rather fit Horse Guard trotting up The Mall towards Buckingham Palace. As it stopped inside the inner most enclosure, I alighted to be greeted on the front steps by Helen Mirren as Queen Elizabeth. As I lifted from my curtsy she said, 'It's a great honour you know. You'll be able to put your drag prices up after this. Remember... it's Ma'am as in spam, not Ma'am as in farm. She's American you know.' American? She signalled to an emissary to take me inside.

'This way dear!' he teased and minced off up a long golden corridor.

'What's this all about?' I whispered.

'Well... oh no I can't!' he giggled. 'I'm sworn to secrecy. Sworn I am, sworn. Secrecy is my middle name. No I won't tell. I mustn't!' As we turned a corner, I heard a gruff shout from behind.

'Oi!' I turned to see Princess Margaret, sitting in a wheelchair draining another shot from a Gordon's Gin optic mounted to the wall beside her. 'Don't put her in yellow for fuck's sake,' she drawled, 'It'll clash with her teeth!'

After lingering momentarily to watch Prince Harry do press-ups wearing nothing but Calvin Klein underpants and boots, we stopped outside a huge red and golden door.

'Now remember,' said the emissary, 'It's Merm as in sperm, not Mame as in Lucille Ball.' He dropped to one knee with arms outstretched and sang, 'Everything's coming up drag shoes and lollipops!'

'That was Ethel Merman in Gypsy, you stupid queen!' I scolded. With a disgruntled sigh he threw open the doors and there she was... soon to be Queen herself, Catherine Middleton the Great. I attempted a curtsy but bumped into the emissary and collapsed at the base of a busy-lizzy jardinière. Kate looked a fright. Her hair was tied up in shards of white fabric and she wore what can only be described as an army fatigue kaftan with Princess Diana souvenir slippers on her feet. I stood for a moment in awe of the normality of it all.

'Now look here,' she growled in a deep Texan drawl. 'If I'm gonna be Queen one day, there's gonna be a few changes around here!' I was a little taken aback that our future queen wasn't English as we had all been led to believe. I guess this was how the nation had felt about Mrs Simpson.

'How do you mean, sperm... Mame... sorry I mean Ma'am?' I stuttered.

'Well it's all too twee and British. What this town needs is a little Vegas. There's too much old Queen and not enough drag queen. And that's why I called you!'

I violently awoke from my dream in a cold sweat. I glanced across at Charlie, who was sound asleep. I got up and had a cigarette. There I was sitting in the dark pondering this imaginary crisis like my life depended on it. 'This is stupid!' I said to myself and went back to bed.

'I think you had a little turn, dear!' said the emissary, standing over me smiling. Bollocks… I was back in the same dream! I jumped to my feet. The soon to be Queen Catherine continued.

'The first problem we have to deal with is this.' She ripped open the Velcro down the front of her kaftan to reveal she was eight months pregnant.

'Bugger!' I cried.

'If I'd agreed to that when he asked, I wouldn't be in this mess now, would I?' she explained, taking a long draw on her Cuban cigar. 'I need a wedding dress in a hurry. Urgently. You're a drag queen, think of something!' My head was spinning with responsibility. Three billion people would be watching this wedding and I needed a solution fast.

'Erm…' I gulped. 'Perhaps a meringue ball gown like the one Deborah Kerr wore in The King and I?'

'Go on…' Kate quizzed.

'Well, if we Empire line it from under the bust, it would cover the bump.' She smiled.

'Let's do it. There's a sewing machine over there and as much help as you need. Come on people!' She yelled, clapping her hands. 'Let's go! Let's make this happen!'

Moments later, I was joined at the sewing machine by a squadron of military men... cutting fabric, fluffing feathers and hand-sewing beads and sequins, as I ran meter after meter of gold lamé under the needle. In the background the music from the Countdown clock ticked the seconds. Within minutes, the frock was finished. It took six squaddies to help her put it on.

'You'll be needing this, dear' said the emissary, handing me a small remote control device. I pressed the button and Kate's tits began flashing like beacons at either end of a zebra crossing.

'Nooooo!' she screamed. Suddenly from under the front of her skirt leapt the Queen Mother. She took a flying run at me and punched me in the chops. I awoke with Charlie's arm across my face. I decided I wouldn't be watching the Royal Wedding after all. I didn't think I could stand the stress!

SUNSET ESCAPE

It was the phone call I'd been dreading. 'I'll be at yours at ten am.'

'I'm sorry I can't I'll be busy,' I bluffed.

'But I'm only in town for one day before I go back to Manchester. Can't you get out of whatever it is you're doing?' The truth was I had absolutely nothing planned at all. But Bobby had won a sunshine escape to Madrid off the back of a cornflake packet and was desperate to show me the photos… yawn. I'd previously made a decision not to rise to his gloating and ignore the phone as soon as I saw his number, but I'd been distracted with a bit of celery stuck between my front teeth and got caught out.

'I erm… I've got an audition,' I said, trying to hold the phone between my ear and shoulder while flicking to the employment column of The Stage And Television Today newspaper to find my alibi. It was no use making anything up, Bobby would check.

'Sunset Boulevard… yes that's it. Open auditions.' He put the phone down on me. Now he'd be off to the newsagent to buy his own copy of the paper to confirm my story. It also meant he would most likely be waiting outside to see if I arrived. If I didn't go, he would attempt to humiliate me as a liar to everyone I know. It would save me a lot of grief if I just turned up, waited until he left, then went shopping.

The auditions were taking place in a small theatre currently closed for redecoration, just off the main run through Holborn. I turned the corner to the entrance just in time to see someone emptying their breakfast to the side of the main stairs. Stage fright can be a terrible thing. Sure enough, in the window of a coffee shop opposite sat Bobby. He was wearing dark glasses in a vague attempt to remain hidden. I obliged by pretending not to see him and entering the theatre foyer.

The main lobby was a paddock of stage-school cattle to the slaughter, all singing and reciting and leaping about in preparation. One girl was teetering meditatively on her head while another was clutching one of the marble statues, desperately attempting to stretch one leg high onto its shoulder. The statue's face frowned in disapproval. A little group of aspiring starlets sat on the floor chatting. They all stopped and looked at me. Perhaps I appeared as alien as I felt.

'Hello, I'm Alisha Du Barry. I've not seen you before. Why don't you join us?' said one of the wannabe's, offering a choreographed willowy hand gesture. I sat in a small space as close to the exit as was possible. She tediously introduced her troupe, taking time on each girl's name, credentials and resume.

'And you are?'
'Jeff Kristian.'
'And what do you do Jeff Kristian?'
'I'm a singer… and drag queen.' There was a moment's excited silence.

'Wow! That's fantastic!" lisped her friend Kristy-Anne Lowther, who'd apparently done a "woman with dog" in The Bill and was "second girl at bus stop" in a TV pilot that was almost guaranteed to be shown in the Autumn.

'Why didn't you come in drag?'

'For Sunset Boulevard?' I questioned.

'Sweetie, you're missing the point. You need to stand out from the crowd, be remembered. Look!' she said, pointing to her feet. She was wearing one green sock and one red.

'Why are you wearing odd socks?' I asked.

'They're not odd, look Lindsay Le-Crosse is wearing the same!' They all laughed. 'Actually, we swap socks when we arrive. To be noticed by the panel. They remember the girl with the green and red socks.' And there was me thinking they'd remember the girl who had talent.

'How does that work if Lindsay Le-Crosse is wearing the same?'

'No silly, I'm the girl with the green and red socks and she's the girl with the red and green socks!' Indeed, how could I be so silly? The whole cackle found this highly amusing, so much so that a part of Kristy-Anne Lowther's tooth retainer came loose and flicked a piece of her half-devoured apple into someone's drink. This was more torturous than the prospect of Bobby and his photos! I politely made my excuses to leave, saying I needed to find a toilet. I made my way to the exit but Bobby was still staring from across the road. The wannabees were still staring from behind me, too. With yet another lie to back up, I followed a sign to the loos.

I had to wait a few minutes to get a free urinal. There was a second queue behind several boys faffing in front of a small wall mirror. The man in the mirror was having trouble applying a second coat of mascara whilst the chap over his shoulder appeared to be equally traumatised by his long floppy fringe. I reached the front of my queue and unbuttoned my fly.

'Have you ever gone down on one of these?' came a deep, commanding theatrical voice to my right.

'I... I'm sorry?' I stuttered, almost afraid to look.

'This,' he said, pointing to some sort of exercise contraption leaning against the wall under his urinal. 'I find it great for perfect abs. See?' He turned towards me and parted his audition-ready open shirt. He did indeed have perfect abs. Though it was a little difficult to concentrate on his stomach while his pants were still down around his thighs.

'Ooh let me see!' said a softer voice to my left. I wasn't sure which bit of equipment he was referring to, but either way it was impossible for me to step back out of the way whilst still in mid-flow.

Finally reaching the sink to wash my hands, a tall painfully thin man asked, 'What do you think of this hat? Too Machiavellian?' I wasn't sure what Machiavellian meant.

'Smashing,' I encouraged, looking at my watch. I'd been there for two hours. If Bobby was still sitting opposite, I could tell him I'd done the audition by now, so I decided to leave. But I got home to find him sitting on my doorstep clutching a photo album. I'd wasted all that time faffing about with bloody Sunset bastard Boulevard and didn't escape anything. Just shows it doesn't pay to tell fibs.

GOING THROUGH THE BINS

I was ready to punch someone. No particular individual, just anyone. I'd had the morning from hell and was fed up with the life I was leading. I stormed into Pret A Manger like a menstruating tornado and then headed with my take-away to commune with nature in Soho Square. After a few deep breaths and some considerable cursing, I felt a little better. It was after all such a sunny day. I attempted to perch resplendently on a wooden bench as if defying the knot of anxiety in my stomach. I felt like Snow White surrounded by birds and small fury animals, all staring intensely at my sandwich as I took it from the bag.

Across the way under the dappled light from the huge majestic trees, I could see an old codger going through one of the bins. He wore a tatty coat and a woollen hat with fingerless gloves despite the glorious weather. Stopping for a moment he looked up at me, squinting in the sunlight. He then made a beeline towards me. My heart sank at the thought of my much-needed calm being disturbed. Still, on the bright side, perhaps he would be the person I could punch.

Sitting himself on the bench beside me he said, 'What a remarkable day!' I felt a brief shudder of shame over my surprise at how well-spoken he was.

'I haven't got any money!' I curtly scolded.
'Neither have I so that makes us equal,' he smiled. 'Would you mind if I took my lunch with you?' He

pulled a half-eaten lump of something from his pocket to show me as if to demonstrate he wouldn't be after mine. I reluctantly nodded my approval. 'I've seen you here a few times before,' he said taking a big bite. Well, I say bite… it was more a suck and tear as he didn't have many teeth.

'Have you?' This was a bit stalkerish for me so early in the conversation.

'Yes, because I live here.'

'What… in the park? I haven't noticed you here before.'

'Probably because you are usually too distracted by your own thoughts. Look!' He pointed to a stout woman in an ill-fitting pink flowery dress sitting opposite. She was negotiating a vast clutch of paper sandwich bags balanced precariously on her lap whilst trying at the same time to read a magazine. As we watched, her phone rang. She angrily switched it off and lobbed it into the handbag by her side. Calmly brushing the lank hair from her face, she took a bite from an enormous baguette. As she bit into one end a lump of something fell from the other onto her lap, followed swiftly by a hungry pigeon. She panicked and the remainder of her filling fell out, much to the delight of a further dozen birds who descended upon her like locusts.

I was shocked. 'Aw my Gawd, is that me? Is that how I am?' Having been forced to notice the world beyond my own bubble, I took a closer look. There was a tall skinny woman trying to prise something from the bottom of her shoe without stopping walking, falling over or dropping her coffee. There was an oriental man picking his nose while arguing on a mobile. And a constantly sneezing man with a fat little squirrel which slowly but deliberately edged its way closer and closer to a piece of discarded food at his feet. But every time it got close, he sneezed again and the poor little rodent legged it.

'What about you?' I asked the tramp. 'Surely you don't like living like this?'

'This is my life,' he pronounced. My mind flitted briefly to the Dame Shirley Bassey song of the same name. I tried to imagine her in a rancid overcoat and fingerless gloves going through the bins. 'This is how I chose to live. I own nothing, owe nothing, and have no worries or ties. I don't even know the time or what day it is. My life is divided into four... Spring, Summer, Autumn and Winter. That's all I need to know.'

'Yes, but with the greatest respect... picking through rubbish?'

'I merely recycle the things that other people don't want anymore.'

I could see logic in what he was saying, though I'm not sure I could live that way. But I suppose we have to make the best of what we have. Just looking around I could see I wasn't the only one coping with stress. I realised that we never really know the backstory of people we share our parks with; what circumstances created their "now". Was it better to live a life of blinkered high tension, or just chill and enjoy the world around you whilst going through the bins?

HALLOWEEN HUMBUG

I can't be doing with Halloween. Pumpkins with bits hacked out to make a ghoulish face. Fake cobwebs clogging up me air conditioning. Cardboard cut outs of skeletons and candles carved to look like Dickens' ghosts. Cauldrons, broomsticks… wall posters of Donatella Versace… And if you're gonna be an evil witch, why do it for just one day of the year? With Christmas decorations in the shops from August, I say just throw the tree up early and skip Halloween altogether.

One All Hallow's Eve many years ago I was working with my gorgeous drag sister, the fabulous Miss Julie Paid. She'd got a booking near Portsmouth at eight and I'd got one in Brighton at midnight. So we'd decided to save on petrol, travel in the same charabang and double-act on each, leaving on the same face of makeup between the two shows. The journey down to the south coast began well. We were on schedule, which made a change for us. Singing merrily along to a collection of dead people on eight track and tooting the horn every time we saw a shaggable lorry driver. But as night fell, so did a creepy dense fog.

Suddenly through the haze there appeared on the side of the road a hitchhiker. He had a look of Jean Claude Van Damme so I though it only polite to offer a lift, what with the weather and all.

'What are you doing?' screamed Julie as I chugged to a halt on the hard shoulder.

'Stopping to offer that young man relief,' I replied.

'Are you mad? He could have a blood-stained axe in that bag. Besides which he's wearing corduroy. Drive on!' Ready to wheel spin away like Kelly Garrett from Charlie's Angels, I turned to look back but Jean Claude had mysteriously vanished.

'Ooh, he's took me all of a quiver!' I shuddered.

'In your dreams!' Julie retorted. A little unnerved we continued to Portsmouth, finding comfort in the possibility that we hadn't seen a ghost, he'd probably just fallen in a ditch on his way to the car.

The first venue was a huge hotel smack bang in the middle of fuckin' nowhere. Glancing over the top of my Jackie O's, all I could see was Dracula's Castle. Expecting Riff Raff from the Rocky Horror Show to greet us at the door, we clacked across the vintage cobbles and up the stairs to the austere stone pillared entrance. We were doing a Stag Night. Just us and a group of straight blokes, pissed up and pissed off that Julie Paid wasn't a female stripper. The show was a disaster; it went down like a pork sausage in a Synagogue. I grabbed our fee and we were back in that car before the echo from my handbag snapping shut had faded.

But the fog was getting denser. And there was an eerie silence on the road with not another car for miles. Yes, we were lost. And running rather late. Worse still, neither of our mobiles could pick up a signal. Suddenly out of nowhere, we saw a deserted petrol station on the opposite side of the road. Leaving Julie with the car, I jogged across to get directions. There wasn't a tortured soul in sight, other than a heavy woman in a pink and red shell suit snoring at the till behind the security window. Tapping at the glass with a lucky sixpence had no effect. So I tried banging hard with the flat of my hand. She awoke with a start, looked up at my full face of drag makeup through the glass and let out a blood-curdling scream that would have made Hammer Horror proud. Her wheelie chair shot backwards and she fell with a crash to the floor, taking a large wire display rack of sweets with her. Smarties flew from their tubes in all directions across the floor and a pile of Cadbury's Flakes landed in her lap. I have to confess, I was a tad shocked myself. She began hyperventilating and clutching her chest.

'Oh my God, I'm so sorry,' I said. 'You're not having a heart attack are you?'

'No, you've made my tits hurt,' she gasped. 'It's a new braaaaaa...' she explained, bursting into tears. I'd only wanted directions back to the M23, not a run down on the state of her udders. 'Oh it's alright, I was getting bored anyway,' she sobbed, subconsciously un-wrapping her first Flake.

Twenty minutes of therapy and three more chocolate bars later, it was clear we wouldn't make it to the Brighton show on time, so we didn't bother trying. Though it took us four hours to get home through the fog. Halloween? Bah, humbug!

IN THESE SHOES?

'It'll end in tears,' said my partner Charlie with a tone of dread in his voice. He wasn't far wrong. Usually a Ladies Night performance would be myself as drag host, Charlie as musical director, perhaps two male strippers and an audience of about fifty to a hundred or so women. But this booking was something else! Billed as the biggest girlie treat of the century may have sounded a bit opulent for Portsmouth, but it was probably true. There would be seven of our exotic boys, a Blues Brothers tribute show and no less than four hundred frantic, frisky twenty-to-thirty-something year-old women drinking Champagne all night. In addition to this, there would be an Ann Summers lingerie fashion show and six Chippendale table-service waiters, all of whom also needed dressing room space. And the entire event was to be managed and hosted by myself and Charlie, with assistance from the daft agent who created the whole stupid idea. No run-through, no dress rehearsal, just turn up on time and get on with it. Hmm.

The night before, I sat with a strong glass of Gordon's and a pen and paper. Taking into account the flow of the show, I would need fourteen costumes, fourteen wigs, fourteen pairs of shoes and about a hundred-weight of jewellery. I also packed plenty of hairspray, several pairs of tights and plenty of Alka-Seltzer.

'I don't know how we're going to fit all of this into a three-and-a-half-hour show,' I said to Charlie the next day.

'Never mind that, I don't know how we're gonna fit all this into the car!' he replied. But fit it he did and we were underway.

The venue for this mad-cap extravaganza was a huge nightclub attached to a Hotel on Southsea waterfront. We had set out early to allow enough time to get in and set everything up. Sound check complete, we went for a wander along the esplanade. It was very cold, and a bitter wind seemed to find every little gap in my clothing, though the fresh air was invigorating after a long-cramped car journey. We returned to the venue at seven, the doors would open at eight and the show would begin at eight-thirty. But seeing a queue of eager women, the inexperienced nightclub manager had opened the doors at six. A hundred girls were already throwing Champagne down their necks two and a half hours before the show was even due to start. This was going to be a disaster!

'Ooh, you're sexy ain't ya?' said one lusty broad, running across the woodblock to Charlie. 'Are you one of the strippers?' she slobbered, rubbing his shaven head.

'No, get away woman!' he replied.

'Aw, but I love skinheads,' she drooled.

'So do I, piss off!' Charlie wasn't happy. And we hadn't even started. The Ann Summers girls pulled in, smart and professional and with the sensible decision that there was to be no fashion show, just a stand at the back of the hall. Eight-thirty arrived... but none of the other performers had, with the exception of half the Blues Brothers act. The women were getting impatient and rowdy, so we decided to get things underway with some jokes and a few songs. Mid-song, one of the strippers arrived. But instead of directing him to the stage door, the nightclub manager sent him through the auditorium. Pandemonium broke out. It was like a scene from St. Trinians. As he escaped back stage, one hapless drunk clinging desperately onto the back of his jacket tripped on the steps and threw up across the front of the stage. While someone searched for a mop and bucket, we sat in the dressing room with the stripper. He was horrified, sweating and shaking.

'They're out of control. I wouldn't like to be in your shoes!' he stuttered.

'These things often look better on paper,' I replied. Suddenly the agent arrived. He was stoned and handed me a tatty, scrunched up scribbling of paper which had apparently started its life as a running order for the show. He seemed to think this was very funny and giggled endlessly, especially as he'd forgotten to tell us I was also supposed to be hosting a male slave auction. Charlie swung into gear, evicted him to the bar and got the show underway. It appeared we had at last created some sort of order out of chaos. Three more strippers had meanwhile turned up and were now getting ready, the arrival of the Chippendale waiters meant all the girls could remain seated and somewhat more controllable, and the rest of the Blues Brothers were ready to perform.

Everything was running like clockwork, nobody dared argue with Charlie and all was well. That is until the third stripper's fire-eating act set off the evacuation alarms. We had to negotiate four hundred drunken women onto the front lawn, where we were joined by three hundred irritable hotel guests; awoken from their slumber and hurriedly flung out to group behind the bushes, still in pyjamas and nighties. My sing-along crowd control efforts worked well… until twenty firemen arrived! Of course, it was a false alarm. The funniest sight of the evening was watching four hundred women in six-inch stilettos trying to run at the fire boys across a muddy lawn. The scariest sight was twenty minutes later, seeing each fireman climbing back into his engine wearing one of my wigs lifted from the dressing room.

The agent phoned me the next day to congratulate us on our efforts. Same again next year? In these shoes? I don't think so!

EXMAS, INNIT?

As a rule, I like to get Easter out of the way before I start getting ready for Christmas. I am of course being ironic. It seems that preparations for the festive season are beginning earlier and earlier, year by year. The first TV advert in the UK that mentions Christmas tends to be in June. I'm not going to out a particular advertiser here, but suffice to say that if there are any potential customer out there who need reminding they've only got six months to have their new settee in place for the last week of the year, they're probably not the sort of moron who should be given interest free credit with nothing to pay for two years. Unless of course, the intention is to rip off the easily led.

I think it's that feeling of being force fed Christmas that I find so unsettling. It's not that many years ago that it was all so different. We'd have whatever kind of summer we could scrape together in Britain with more rain and cloud than sunshine, and then autumn would begin. We'd wrap up warmer and get a little cosier. Bonfire night would be a treat with a few fireworks, if the nation's animals didn't get too stressed with all the noise. Then we'd begin looking forward to the decorations going up just a couple of weeks later. But Christmas is now with us for six months every year, and I no longer feel I have it to look forward to. No sooner has it gone away than it's back again. Dreaming of a white Christmas when… August?

'Duh... it's because of the recession!' explained Shawn the Shop Assistant, in a manner suggesting I'd been in a time capsule for the past ten years.

'Hmm... go on,' I suggested, expectantly.

'Well, obviously the shops gotta start selling Exmas gear earlier-like cause no-one's got any money, innit?' I'm sure he understood his own logic, though I wasn't sure I did. Though I did manage to stop myself punching him for calling Christmas "Exmas." I even managed to hold back when he said he'd go and "arksk" his Manager. I was just thinking what an idiot he was, when the back of my shoulder bag caught on an oversized, over-decorated Christmas tree next to the counter. It fell forward and emptied its baubles and accoutrements over an area the size of a small car park. Thankfully I managed to "ekskape" the store before Shawn and his Manager returned.

On the drive home I pondered what had happened. To this teenage shop boy, it had seemed perfectly normal. But then, this was probably all he had ever known. Maybe it was just me being old. Perhaps the thing to do was to embrace the change and try to accept that yuletide decorations in the shops are OK in September. Time goes on, things progress...

'What the hell is that digging in my back?' A quick fumble inside my coat and I pulled out a small plastic reindeer, no doubt a remnant of my encounter with the tree in the shop. Distracted for a moment, I mounted the grass bank to the side of the road and ran into something. Shame washed over me, followed quickly the horror that I may perhaps have hit an animal. With my heart in my throat, I leapt from the car. I'd actually run into a plastic tube, positioned to protect a small sapling from the elements until it had strengthened. The tree had snapped off at ground level. I picked it up; it was like a tiny Christmas tree. And even though it was still only September, I felt a nostalgic sadness. The fact that it looked like a Christmas tree was somehow worse than if it had been any other. I held it up. In my other hand I still had the small reindeer, strangely to the same scale as the poor baby tree. Unable to cast it aside, I rushed back to the car with it before anyone could see what I'd done.

Back at home, I found a small terracotta pot in the garden and filled it with sand. In it, I sat the Christmas tree. I found some tinsel in the cupboard under the stairs, but it was way too big for the miniature branches, so I trimmed it with scissors before draping. I added a couple of glittery feathers from my costume sewing-box. On the front just inside the rim of the pot, I sat the little reindeer. If anyone had ever suggested I'd have a tree up in September, they'd definitely have been taken off my Christmas card list. And yet though embarrassed to admit it, now I had one I quite liked it. Maybe I should've arksked the baby Jesus for forgiveness... innit tho?

IT'S A MAN THING

Charlie was building a shed. In a far-flung corner of our garden in Kent there was a gap and I was told that gap needed to be filled. It's a man thing. And when your man gets one of these primeval home-building ideas in his head there's nothing you, as a Shed Widow, can do.

'I think it looks quite nice with a gap there,' I suggested. But that was the wrong answer and the decision had already been made. In the middle of the night I found him standing in the garden in the dark looking at this gap. His head buzzing with this machismo project, he couldn't even sleep. 'What about a nice tree? Or something that flowers, like a Rhododendron?' But apparently, I didn't understand because the bottom of the garden is male territory. I always thought it was for faeries. I went back to bed.

I awoke early the following morning with a start, to something that sounded like the east wing collapsing. I leapt out of bed and looked out of the window. Once the immense dust cloud cleared, I could see a Wickes Building Supplies lorry tipping a ton of gravel. This was getting serious now… the windows would need cleaning again!

After making coffees, I found Charlie in the gap digging a huge hole. The gravel was hard-core for the foundation apparently, and the huge pile of wood that came with it was going to be the shed itself. I needed more caffeine. By the back door was a collection of Wickes bags with all sorts of man things poking out. I sat on the doorstep in my slippers and dressing gown with my second coffee, having a rummage. There was an array of brackets, hinges, wire and bulkhead lighting. Then I found something quite shocking. It was a bag of Galvanised Clout Nails. Now where I come from, a "clout" is a common euphemism for the female private parts, which I as a drag queen of course found highly amusing. By the time Charlie arrived for his second coffee I was crying with laughter, so much so that I couldn't explain why. He of course thought I was laughing at him and his shed and stormed back up the garden in disgust. Oh dear!

I got dressed and met him at the gap with a third coffee. 'I wasn't laughing at you, you know. It was just them Galvanised Clout Nails. Is it the clout that galvanised or just the nails?'

'It's for getting felt on the roof,' he replied seriously. I guessed he was referring to fixing down the shed's waterproof covering and not a quick grapple in full view of the neighbours. I bit my bottom lip and decided not to say anything. But the gap was no longer a gap... it now had a concrete floor.

My dear friend Amber found it all so amusing, sitting with me on the patio in her wide-brimmed hat and sunglasses with her long glass of Pimms.

'There's an awful lot of hammering,' she said taking a long drag on one of her Gauloises. 'Darling I don't know why you put up with it. Let me take you shopping. Laura Ashley have moved to a new shop and I hear it's frightful.' She stopped mid-sentence, suddenly distracted. 'Who the fuck's that?' Peering over her glasses, she pointed at the elderly man from next door, staring intently at Charlie over the top of the six-foot fence.

'That's Mr Jones. He looks very angry doesn't he? Perhaps it's all the noise.' I didn't want to upset the neighbours, so I popped round to see Mrs Jones.

'Don't worry Jeff dear, it's not the noise. It's the competition. If your Charlie's having a shed, then he wants one as well. You know what they're like, it's best to let them just get on with it.'

By the time I got back to mine, there was hammering from next-door's garden too.

'You've got him building one now!' I told Charlie. War was officially declared, and the race was on to see which man could finish first.

'How delicious!' declared Amber. 'I wonder how Mr Jones is getting on. Let's take a look from an upstairs window,' she suggested gleefully.

'It's a bungalow, you silly bitch!' I replied. 'But I do know where there's a hole in the fence.' Amber removed her stilettos before we climbed into the hedgerow. Mr Jones was a little ahead of Charlie on account that he'd already had a concrete base left over from something else. Amber fell into the privet and the fence wobbled. It was leaning towards the Jones'. I then saw that Mr Jones had the side of his new creation tied to one of our fence posts with a bit of rope. He was cheating and Charlie was furious.

'I'll finish before that bastard if it's the last thing I ever do!' But as Charlie's hammering speeded up, so did Mr Jones'. It was gonna be a race to the death!

'I was due at Margeurite's barbecue by half past, but this is far more entertaining, so I think I'll stay,' announced Amber. 'Besides, all this rampant testosterone in the air is rejuvenating for a woman of my age.' It would have taken more than testosterone to rejuvenate that, I mused. But it wasn't unusual for Amber to invite herself to tea.

After a while, Charlie approached grinning like the Cheshire Cat from Alice In Wonderland. 'It's finished!' he announced, in a voice loud enough to carry next door. Amber was confused.

'Darling, it's very pretty but it hasn't got any walls. Shouldn't a shed have walls?'

'It's a gazebo!' Charlie responded proudly.

'Oh darling, how frightfully clever. Here, have a Pimms. Congratulate yourself!'

'Mr Jones will be devastated,' I said.

'So will his shed when I cut that rope off our fence and it collapses,' smiled Charlie smugly. 'But all is fair in love and war. I'll at least wait till he's finished.'

TROUBLE AT MILL

It really was too good an opportunity to miss. I'd been working so hard, and a well-earned break would do me good. And best of all, it was all paid for by someone else. Donald and Crisco had planned to go to Holland with their friend Martin, but at the last minute he'd had some kind of crisis with his pet parakeet. Aptly named Rover, it had indeed wandered off through an open window. Rover had done this before and made his way back a few days later no worse for wear. Nonetheless, Martin was understandably beside himself with worry and had therefore decided to stay at home and wait for his prodigal overgrown budgie's return. So Donald and Crisco had invited me to go in his place. Under normal circumstances, pride alone would usually stop me from being a second choice backup plan for anyone. After all, they could have invited me first instead of Martin. However, I was knackered and any chance of a free holiday was not to be sniffed at.

From the ferry we took a train into Amsterdam Centrum. Travelling light for just a weekend, it was an easy twenty-minute walk to the hotel. Once booked in, it was just a matter of deciding how to spend our time. Crisco had spent most of the train journey shocking us with tales of his last trip to Amsterdam. He was nicknamed after a well-known American brand of cooking grease, often used as one of the more heavy-duty sexual lubricants amongst a certain type of gay fraternity. So it wasn't too much of a… shall we say "stretch" of the imagination to guess at his plans. He advised us of every nook and cranny of a plethora of seedy, dark and dingy dungeon-like venues he'd found on his previous trip. It was quite fascinating to see a side of him I hadn't known before. The poor love wore himself out with all the anticipation and had to sleep for the second half of the journey. Donald and I on the other hand had decided to have a bash at culture.

We took a trip on a canal boat that promised to "drift through the famous open flower fields of Holland, the centre of Europe's bloom industry." I think drift was a bit of an understatement. We picked up quite a speed over most of the trip. In fairness, it was quite late in the day. Donald and I had decided that the man driving the boat was probably late for his tea. Despite this, it was one of the most beautiful sights I think I've ever experienced. It put me in mind of a young Judy Garland in the Wizard of Oz, falling asleep in the field of flowers. Luckily for us, there were no flying monkeys in Holland.

    Next, we had decided to visit a windmill. Back in town, some tiny little woman wearing dungarees and covered in piercings had handed us a promotional flyer. We were a little disgruntled at first when the taxi drove us back out into the same countryside we had just returned from. But being aliens, we decided to laugh it off for now and just plan better the next day.

I've seen many windmills before from a distance. But you don't realise how big windmills really are until you stand right up next to one. We were told this was a working windmill. However, the guide was wearing traditional Dutch dress with a huge white hat, necktie and clogs, so it was unclear whether she meant working as in "still producing" or working as in "not broken". The inside was cavernous. Completely made of wood and over four floors, each linked with a wonky wooden staircase that wound itself up around the inside of the building. We decided to explore the whole place, but the further up the building we got, the more it seemed to sway from side to side as the enormous sails went around.

'This doesn't feel safe, does it?' Donald said, a little freaked out.

'Well it says in the leaflet that it's been here for a hundred and fifty years, so don't worry,' I tried to comfort. He seemed oddly stressed.

'Yes but they always say things like that, as though it will be here another hundred and fifty years. But supposing it was only built to last a hundred and fifty years and this is its last day?' He had a point, though he did appear to be over-reacting a little.

We finally reached the top. Donald was now panting. When I looked at him, his neck had swollen like a bullfrog. He suddenly had the appearance of something from The Exorcist. 'My God, what happened to your face?' I cried.

'It's my wheat allergy!' he croaked, gasping for breath.

'Wheat allergy?' I gasped. 'And we're visiting a Windmill? Are you mad? Why didn't you say anything? Give me strength!' Close to collapse, his knees began to buckle, and I knew I needed help to get him out of there. By the time I had run down four flights of stairs to get the guide, then ran all the way back up again, and then helped the guide carry Donald back down, I needed an ambulance myself. I spent the remainder of our break in a clinic at Donald's bedside waiting for his face to become human again. Needless to say, Crisco was nowhere to be found. So much for a free holiday! That'll teach me to be greedy.

PETALS OF FORTUNE

I like to bathe in rose petals. It's not a romantic thing particularly, and now and again it can be a nuisance. On more than one occasion it's taken ten minutes to get the loose fragments out of all my crevices with a towel. But I persevere because I can tell my fortune by the petals. A dear friend told me about it some time ago.

My first attempt was a bit of a disaster. She didn't explain I had to remove the petals from the plant first... the thorns and roots scratched me to buggery. But now I've got the hang of it, a window to my future is there for me every time I do it. It's the nearest thing to reading tea leaves, only instead of just your lips touching the liquid, it's your whole body so, in theory, more accurate. When you drain away the water, the nearer the plughole the petals settle the worse the news. And like tealeaves, you look at the pictures the petals make. For example, if you see an anchor it means you're going on a voyage. A baby means new beginnings, though it could mean something else if you're a breeder. A sword means strength, a snake means health (like the famous apothecary serpent used by chemists), and so on. If it all just clumps over the plughole it means you've left it too long to have a bath, so do it more often. If you just keep seeing pictures of your Mother, you probably need therapy.

I saw a picture of a car near the plughole just before someone let our tyres down. Once I even saw a picture of Lesley Joseph. Two days later my partner Charlie and I met her in the NCP Car Park in Soho's Chinatown. But readers beware… it might not always be good news!

Some time ago, I was due to go to a script reading for a part in an Old Time Music Hall revue. Though it would be mostly singing, there was some speaking, so a read-through was essential. It was undecided whether I should play Tommy Trinder or Marie Lloyd in drag… all the more reason to read.

I was a little nervous, so the night before I had decided on a rose petal bath to see if it gave me any tips. As the water subsided and the petals settled, I could see two things. The first was a shoe. Could this be symbolic of the part I would take? One of the reasons it had been suggested I read for Marie Lloyd as a drag queen was that I was one of only two people in the Company who could prance in high heels. Prancing was apparently required in three different songs, so not a job for someone who could only shuffle. The other prancer was a rather plump girl called Sally. Not only did a few of the other cast members not like her very much but some considerable work would need to be undertaken in letting out and enlarging the old costume from the previous year. And Linda the costume mistress was particularly unhappy about this as she'd made the seams very small so as to have enough of the donated fabric left to secretly do new curtains for her downstairs cloak. Sally being Marie Lloyd would mean she'd have to create three rhomboid parallelogram gussets and thus lose her beloved curtains. Though as Roger pointed out, she'd still have the pelmet and could recycle one of the tiebacks as a coaster for the vase on the windowsill.

The other rose petal picture in my bath was a table lamp. I wasn't too sure what this could mean at first, but finally decided it symbolised a new idea. Like when a light bulb appears above a cartoon character's head to demonstrate they have a cunning plan. The problem was that both pictures were kind of half way up the bath, so I couldn't tell whether they were good or bad. I lost a night's sleep over this dilemma, but by the morning I had decided over toast and marmalade to head off in good spirits with optimism, despite being so tired.

Though it was after rush hour, the tube was still quite busy. I had managed to find a seat by the second stop, but my lack of sleep began to take effect. I couldn't stop yawning and my head was bobbing in and out of consciousness like a nodding dog on a parcel shelf. At one station a few seconds after the doors had opened, I suddenly realised I'd gone one stop past where I should. I lunged at the doors and managed to jump through just as they were closing. But my foot caught in the doors behind me and came clean out of my shoe. As the emergency system kicked in and the doors re-opened, my shoe fell down the gap under the train. By the time it had pulled out of the station, my shoe was a chewed-up mess. I limped around on one foot for a while trying to find someone professional to help me retrieve it but to no avail.

I eventually got back to my intended destination and hobbled the two miles or so from the station, arriving over half an hour late. Thankfully this was just a read-through and not a demonstration of my said prancing ability. I pushed through the double doors, expecting to tell my story as predicted in my bath water and to receive lots of sympathetic theatrical lovey air kisses, and perhaps even the offer of a lift back home again. But instead of this longed-for fountain of sympathy, I got Roger. Just Roger. Everyone else had returned home twenty minutes before. Apparently the whole thing had been a production disaster, funding had been pulled at the last minute and the show had had to be cancelled. Or as they say in the world of theatre: lights out.

MEETING THE NEIGHBOURS

I had finally collected the keys on my new third floor flat in Greenwich, close to many of my residential drag shows at the time. I was ready to begin unpacking, but the kitchen was a disgrace. A small room overlooking a courtyard at the back, the wall cupboards were OK but there was a rank smell coming from somewhere under the sink. I opened the cupboard door slowly expecting to find something dead, or perhaps the severed head of the previous tenant's wife. What I found was rot and mould, which extended under the vinyl floor. It all had to be replaced. Luckily I was now living just handbag-lobbing distance from B&Q, so that afternoon I picked up a new sink cupboard and ripped out the old one, getting all the noisy stuff out of the way early in the day so as not to disturb my new neighbours. I had my Ladybird book on Basic Plumbing for Girls to hand and all my tools laid out in the hall. And that evening's show would pay for this gorgeous bit of glitzy pink replacement lino I'd seen on Brixton market. I had everything organised to begin as soon as I got home.

That night with mounting excitement, I propped my book open on page five with a bar of soap found in the top of one of my unpacked boxes. Sticking out from the concrete floor by about an inch was a pipe with the mains water tap to which I had to attach part A. But my heart sank when I noticed that the smell was being caused by water, seeping from underneath the tap. I took my new monkey wrench to tighten the bolt. In an instant the tap flew off and hit me in the middle of the forehead, knocking me flat on my back. The icy cold water from this tiny bit of pipe was now bouncing off the ceiling and showering me. Wiping my eyes, I looked in absolute horror as water spurted in every conceivable direction at an alarming rate. I grappled for the slippery bar of soap now stuck to my book and jammed it onto the end of the pipe. I stood holding it for a moment to get my breath, desperately trying to decide what to do next.

I remembered seeing some old curtains left in the hall cupboard. They would soak up some of the water. But as I took my numbing hand from the bar of soap, the water pressure shot it upwards and out the top window. I ran for the curtains and piled them onto the pipe, which achieved nothing. I needed help, and fast!

With no new phone installed as yet and before mobiles, I desperately banged on the flat next door to use theirs to call a plumber. An elderly man finally answered the door in his blue and white striped pyjamas. He stood bewildered for a moment with his heavily lacquered snow-white comb-over resting on his shoulder rather than his head, looking me up and down. With my long sodden hair hanging across my face, I looked like Esther Williams just out the swimming pool… not that far from the truth.

'Hi, I'm Jeff. I'm your new neighbour,' I said politely, holding out a hand to shake. 'I know its past midnight, but my phone hasn't been connected yet and I've got a bit of an emergency.'

'So I see,' he said looking past me to the puddle of water advancing out of my front door towards the communal stairs. Thankfully he was ex-military and snapping efficiently into action, made the call himself.

Meanwhile, a few more ancient neighbours had begun to appear from other doors around our landing. All in hairnet covered curlers with fluffy slippers and fleeced dressing gowns, they looked at me in disbelief as I introduced myself. It was like the film set of Cocoon but without the vitamins. 'He'll be an hour, so you'll have to block the flow,' commanded the Colonel.

'I was using a bar of soap, but it went out the window,' I said.

'Out the window?!' one of the ladies retorted. It was at that moment I considered abandoning my worldly goods and emigrating to Australia. But with a brave face and some considerable shame, I grabbed an orange from the Colonel's hall table and jammed it over the pipe. There I sat in an icy puddle of orange squash waiting for the plumber, or perhaps better a quick demise from pneumonia. I was distracted briefly by an austere old lady in Wellington boots offering me a cup of tea.

'You'll have to get the caretaker in number three. Press the top bell cause he's deaf and that one rings in his bedroom. The bottom bell's his lounge and he won't hear that from his bed.' We found the mains shut-off at two am behind a panel, behind the wardrobe in the basement flat bedroom. I met sixteen of my new neighbours that night. And the plumber charged me my entire show income. So much for the new lino.

MARY QUANTUM

'It really put the frighteners up me, I can tell you!' said fat Martin. Let me first of all just say that it wasn't me who called fat Martin fat. It may also be appropriate to mention that he wasn't actually fat. He got the nickname because he used to be gargantuan, though thanks to The Britney Spears Vodka and Cocaine Diet Plan, he'd become a rather slender size ten. If anyone asked him why he was called fat Martin, he usually told them it was something to do with girth... I wasn't sure I understood.

He continued, 'I was drinking a beaker of Mellow Birds, and as I brought down the cup it was just standing there grimacing at me like Ena Sharples!' Martin was telling me about the ghost in the haunted shampoo and set booth at his old salon. 'I handed in my notice there and then,' he added. 'My flesh crawls just thinking about it.' Now, fat Martin has been known to be a bit of a drama queen when it comes to stories, but as he stood there quaffing my bouffant, I could see the hairs on his arms standing on end. And I was sitting ten feet away.

'That's that one done, where's your other wig?' he asked.

'Don't worry about that, tell me about this ghost!' I smiled in awe.

'Well, I've been septic to this sort of thing since I had that fling with the gypsy. You remember... he was always talking to spirits.' I remembered he was an alcoholic. 'Until they made him move his caravan out of the car park at the flats. I never saw him again after that, though I do sometimes still sense his presence.' Yes, I also seemed to remember he needed a wash. Them sort of smells can often linger for months. 'Anyway, I think this ghost may be a Victorian barber who used to cut people's throats and sell their flesh to make pies.' Hmm, think I've heard that story before, I thought. But then a couple of months later I saw something on the telly in my kitchen that made me think about Martin and his phantom barber.

The man called it "spooky action at a distance" and said it was all very Alice in Wonderland. Apparently, they did an experiment in Switzerland splitting an atom and sending it in two different directions. They said the two halves of the atom stayed cosmically entwined despite being separated. I had always thought that splitting an atom would create a big explosion. I hastily stopped cutting my carrots and put down my knife. According to the man, not only did it suggest that there are phenomena that can travel faster than light, but that also it may add weight to the possibility that there is an additional dimension other than our own. That our world is just a poor version of the real thing. And that we could for the first time be seeing scientific evidence of a spirit world.

I thought for a moment. It all seemed so profound! But he seemed like quite a nice man, and he was wearing a white coat and glasses, so there must be something in it. But then, a five-dimensional model that includes a perpendicular time to our own, besides the three spatial dimensions could explain these phenomena, I mused. Or am I just being a dizzy

Mary? I took a bite from one of my carrots. Didn't Einstein say that nothing could travel faster than the speed of light? But then didn't Einstein drink his own piss... or was that Sarah Miles? It was all too much. I switched off the telly and went for a lie down.

But I had a terrible nightmare! I dreamt that Sweeney Todd was restyling one of my wigs to look like Helen Shapiro in a YouTube video I'd seen. I had on that lovely pink dirndl frock she'd worn with matching buckled court shoes. He spun me in the chair to look in the mirror... my frock was covered in blood and my hair looked like Albert Einstein, and everyone was laughing. I awoke suddenly in a cold sweat. I had to have a glass of Ribena Toothkind to calm myself down.

I picked up the phone to fat Martin. 'I've just had a terrible dream,' I said, 'it was so intense.'

'What camping?' he asked.

'No, intense... not in tents you dozy bitch! It was about your phantom barber in the shampoo and set room. I've just seen on the telly they reckon there's scientific proof that there really is a spirit world and that that ghost of yours might actually be real.' He was silent for a moment, other than a sniffling sort of sound. 'Are you crying?' I asked.

'No,' he said. 'I'm eating a donut. I've been so depressed. I've put on three stone since I saw you last.'

'Oh Martin, what happened?'

'I was going to the doctor for my depression pills, but the surgery's moved and on the way I passed a cake shop.' There was me worried about Quantum Physics and poor fat Martin could only focus on splitting donut atoms. I invited him round for an emergency Mellow Birds. There was enough in this life to worry about right now. The next life would have to wait.

MOTHER OF MARVIN

Living in the Garden of England as we do, we tend to get a lot of insects visiting the house during the summer. It can upon occasion be a bit of a challenge keeping on top of them. There's never a convenient time to relocate a moth, assuming you can catch him in the first place. I never intentionally kill a creature of any kind. I don't even eat animals and haven't done for thirty-odd years. If you want to get all cosmically political about it, my opinion is that every living being has just as much right to be wherever they are at any given time as I do. And don't even start me on karma! But I will remove them from my home back out to the garden, unless of course they want to pay rent.

Subsequently, we have a dazzling array of equipment for catching all shapes and sizes without harm. The most frequently used is a spare drinking glass to place swiftly over the visitor who is then gently trapped within by a post card of Saint Felix, the patron saint of spiders. I'm not Catholic myself but who's to say the spider isn't, and one does want to do these things properly. Stupidly I'd previously assumed that Saint Felix would be the patron saint of cats until a history teacher friend of mine pointed out that he'd been canonized in seventeen-twelve and that the legendary cartoon cat of the same name didn't first appear until some two hundred years after.

Most creatures I can cope with quite well. But just sitting here writing about spiders makes my blood crawl... how I suffer for my art! This summer in particular has seen a plethora of arachnids in all shapes and sizes like never before. It's as though a package trip coach arrived one night and delivered them all here on holiday from some dark cave somewhere on the continent. A couple of weeks ago, my partner Charlie and I were sitting in front of the telly watching an episode of Upstairs Downstairs. It was the one where Mrs Bridges goes to court for stealing that woman's baby, so quite gripping. Suddenly Charlie cried out and jumped up onto the back of the sofa with fear. 'What?' I asked him, now a little wary myself. He just pointed to a spot on the carpet. Eyes focusing in the darkness, I was horrified to see a spider the size of a fifty pence piece looking back up at me and grinning, teeth glistening in the lamplight. I managed to climb shakily across the coffee table and around the furniture to reach the glass and postcard. As I approached him from behind, he turned to face me, clawing his front leg against the carpet like a prize bull. 'One, two, three...' I cried before rapidly placing the glass over the top of him. Luckily he couldn't count and I had him trapped. 'Come on Marvin I'm not going to hurt you,' I reassured him, sliding Saint Felix's smiling face underneath him. Crisis over we resettled, only to be visited ten minutes later by Marvin's mother! She was the size of the Rock of Gibraltar and definitely looking for her missing son. 'She'll never fit in that glass,' I said turning to Charlie. But Charlie was gone! I rummaged through the cupboards and eventually found a Tupperware bowl large enough to contain her, but when I returned, she too was gone. We hunted for about an hour before finally plucking up the courage to go to bed. We didn't sleep well.

I was yawning a lot on the way to a Ladies Night the following evening. It was quite a small intimate hall of about eighty or so women all buzzing with excitement. I opened my performance with the song Chain Reaction and was about five minutes or so into my run of one-liners when suddenly everyone screamed and pointed in my direction. I looked behind me expecting to see a ghost but there was nobody there. As the room rapidly emptied in panic, I caught a glimpse of something on my shoulder. It was mother of Marvin! She must have hid amongst my costumes and travelled with us in my suitcase. In shock I instinctively knocked her off with my hand. She landed on the floor with a thud and then ran like a thoroughbred into the corner of the room. In reality, she was probably more scared than any of us but, regardless, I was momentarily stunned. Then a little old lady walked over from the entrance. She'd heard the commotion and had had a full report from one tearful girl outside in the hall.

'I'll get the little fellah,' she said gently in a soft Southern Irish drawl, 'Where is it?' I pointed to the danger zone then followed her over.

'Please don't kill it!' I said. She stood for a moment with hands on hips looking down on it.

'Be sure, you wouldn't kill that fecker with a rolling pin!' she laughed, picking it up by the leg. Walking across to an open window she tossed it outside. 'On your way now, then we can get on,' she said to it, wiping her hand on her skirt.

I've often wondered whether Mother of Marvin settled in her new environment or if she was hitchhiking the M20 to get back home to her baby. And how many more would she terrorise along the way?

STARSKY AND CROTCH

'I didn't nick it, it must have just fell in me handbag!' screamed Coleen, taking a swing at the austere looking store detective. I jumped out of the way just in time, as her fist missed its intended target altogether and continued on its course, barely avoiding the tip of my nose. This wasn't the first time she'd been caught shoplifting, though I hadn't previously been with her. After the initial shock of what was occurring, I was filled with shame and embarrassment like I had not known before. Suddenly, a rather large bespectacled man who had been inside stacking the supermarket's shelves just moments before grabbed Coleen by each wrist and pinned her against the outside wall. This wasn't the first time this had happened either, though usually it was under quite different circumstances. I decided to play it naive. I could have just walked away, but my moral obligation to not abandon a friend coupled with a morbid curiosity to see what would unfold had glued me to the spot.

'Can I just ask, what is she accused of stealing?' I asked him.

'She's got a tin of custard in her left-hand pocket and a Curly Wurly stuffed down the front of her knickers,' answered the detective fiercely, reaching into the side of Coleen's coat to retrieve the offending can. This in itself was bad enough, but the day's troubles really began when he tried to reach into her knickers for the Curly Wurly. Coleen head-butted him, making his nose bleed and snapping the bridge of his glasses. Then she kneed the poor shelf stacker in the groin. As he released his grasp and cowered to the pavement in pain, she decided to make a run for it. But she didn't get very far. Looking back to see if she was being followed, quite possibly by me, she didn't notice an old lady's basket on wheels coming out of a shop doorway and tripped, landing in a giant wooden trough planted up with communal flowers. In an instant, she had been apprehended once more by two patrolling community officers.

We had been standing in the freezer section for nearly half an hour and still they couldn't get a confession from Coleen, who was practically foaming at the mouth with rage by this time. My more immediate concern was for my bladder, and the cold from the freezers wasn't helping.

'Do you have a toilet I could use?' I asked innocently.

'You're not going nowhere,' said one of the officers in what was becoming quite close to an American cop show accent. 'You're a witness to this heinous crime and justice must prevail.' I didn't think people spoke like that anymore. And I did think heinous was a bit of an extreme description for someone pinching a tin of custard and a Curly Wurly.

'I didn't see her take anything, I'd have told her to pay for it,' I pleaded. He removed his Starsky and Hutch sunglasses and glared at me.

'Nobody's going anywhere until she confesses,' growled Starsky.

'She doesn't need to confess, they found her with it down her drawers, what other evidence do you need? It's not an Agatha bloody Christie!' I cried. Coleen glared at me with yellow snake eyes. If she could have spat acid she would. I wasn't helping her case, was I? 'Well then would you mind if we move up the aisle a bit out of the freezer section? It's a bit warmer up there by the toilet rolls and bin bags.'

'We're going to have to search you too in a minute, just to be sure you're not an accomplice.'

'Well, I'm going to need to wee before that. If anyone's hand goes down the front of my pants at the moment, I can't promise I won't piss on it!'

'OK come with me,' said the store detective taking my arm and leading me through a swing door to behind the scenes. A desperately needed piddle and a quick pick through my shopping bag later and I was sent home. There was no point waiting for Coleen, she was going to be arrested and taken 'down town', to quote Petula Clark.

I finally got home, exhausted by the events of the afternoon. Slowly I unpacked my own shopping and put it away almost unconsciously. I couldn't get my mind off of what Coleen had done. She was known by everyone to be an attention seeker, but this was usually a means to an end to get someone into bed. If it was a lack of money, I would have gladly stumped up for a tin of Bird's. Maybe it was some kind of obsessive-compulsive disorder, you often hear about it on the telly. My mind back in the room, I looked down to see I was grasping against my chest a packet of three Curly Wurlys that I had bought for myself. I didn't fancy them now, not after the thought of them stuffed down the front of Coleen's crotch. I decided to save them for her the next time she came round for tea. She phoned me a couple of days later to apologise. She had come to terms with what was clearly a problem and had agreed to go to some kind of therapy. For me, shopping in itself is a kind of therapy. Though I have to secretly confess that as much as I care for my dear friend, I will never again go shopping with Coleen.

CHRISTMAS TURKEY

I don't know why I let people talk me into these things. Apparently it was a life and death situation, though I did find that hard to believe. 'She's got a cold and can't sing a note, and if there's nobody on lead the whole extravaganza will be a disaster!' flapped Freddie offering me a vegetarian wine gum.

'Not while I'm driving thanks,' I answered. The snow on the road was thick and slippery and I was having enough trouble without trying to pry a sweet from the sticky mass in his small paper bag.

'You're a professional singer so you're the best person for the job.'

To call it an extravaganza was perhaps a bit of an overstatement. We were due at The Princess Margaret Institute for the Elderly and Infirm on the other side of town to perform a small catalogue of Christmas carols for the residents and staff. Freddie was famous for these yuletide brainwaves, but every time he organised something it was always laced with dilemma, drama and angst. Subsequently, by Christmas day each year he had made himself so ill with worry that he'd been unable to celebrate.

'I do prefer a little rehearsal,' I said, attempting to make him understand that it could all go tits up.

'You know all the songs and I've highlighted your bits in pink,' he said, dangerously thrusting a handful of crumpled song sheets in front of my face. As I pushed them aside, the car skidded and there was a loud thud. 'Oh my God, you've run someone over!' he cried, turning in his seat to look out the back window.

'No it's that frozen turkey of yours in the boot rattling about. It's enormous, we're lucky it didn't knock the wing of the car off.'

'It's a gift for the old folks,' he said charitably.

'I hope they don't want it for this Christmas,' I replied, 'It's gonna take about three months to thaw out!'

As we approached the driveway of the institute, I slowed the car by changing down gear to avoid sliding. But getting off of the busy main road and up the icy slope of the drive was another thing altogether. To avoid disaster before we had even arrived, I drove with one wheel on the snow-covered grass. We held onto the sides of the car as we skated around the back to the boot to get the gift. It was the size of a beach ball and weighed a ton. I wasn't convinced there could be an oven big enough to get it in.

'Perhaps it will shrink a bit when it defrosts?' Freddie sighed optimistically as he struggled to lift it from the car. But alas, his attempt was futile. It slid from his arms like a giant bar of soap and skated at breakneck speed back down the drive and out into the main road, hitting the side of a passing bus. I left Freddie to it and teetered precariously up to the building. Just inside the door was a lectern behind which sat a wrinkled, grey haired man.

'Hello, I'm here to sing carols,' I smiled.

'Ooh smashing, I've been waiting for you,' he said rising to his feet and reaching behind for two crutches. 'Follow me.' His pace was very slow and methodical and made me feel guilty for his trouble.

'If you point me in the right direction, I could find it myself,' I offered.

'No, no. I can do this,' he said lifting one leg onto the bottom of about thirty steps. It occurred to me that I myself had been unsteady on my feet a few moments ago in the snow, but that was just once a year. This poor man was probably like this all the time. It was perhaps a good job he was waiting for me and not the humungous turkey.

At the top of the stairs was a small hall. About fifty metal chairs had been placed facing front, only about six of which were occupied. In the corner by a Christmas tree was a small group of people wearing Santa hats and grasping sheet music.

'Hi, I'm Jeff,' I smiled as I approached them.

'Yes?' asked a short dumpy woman expectantly.

'I'm here to sing lead.' Her smile turned to a frown.

'Well I don't know why,' she gasped with a cough. 'I'm the lead singer in this show. I'm Caroll with two el's,' she snuffled, reluctantly holding out a hand to shake.

'That's appropriate isn't it? Your name's Caroll and you're singing carols?' My attempt to break the ice didn't work. Evidently it was as frosty inside as it was out. Just at that moment, Freddie arrived. Panting and sweating, he ran around the empty chairs to join us.

'What are you doing here Caroll? You said you had a cold, that's why I asked Jeff.'

'I have got a cold,' she sniffed to accentuate the fact. Freddie screwed up my sheet music and turned to face the chairs.

'Where is everyone?' He was close to tears.

'They've all gone upstairs to get their hair done for Christmas,' offered one old man. Caroll with two el's tore off her Santa hat.

'I can't sing in a salon because of the hairspray. It will ruin the purity of my voice.'

'I wouldn't worry love, they've all been on Sherry since breakfast,' came the reply. With a hiss, she stamped her foot and marched out.

All in all, our little Christmas skit went without a hitch. Everyone sang along, though we didn't get much of a standing ovation being as most were in wheelchairs. I'm not sure how many gallons of hairspray I swallowed, but it had been worth the effort. Not such a turkey after all.

TAP SHOE BLUES

It's long been a dream of mine to learn to tap dance. I think it's because I admire it so much in people that have mastered the craft. I'd also been told it was a good way to lose weight. So it was that when I saw a small ad in my local paper, I thought I'd have a go. The piece said, "All levels of experience welcome", so I was comfortable I wouldn't be embarrassed as a complete novice. It also said, "A fun way to keep fit". I had eaten a lot of cake in recent weeks, so perhaps I could kill two birds with one stone and lose a stone from my midriff in the process. I went to a dance shop in town to buy myself the necessary equipment. Tap shoes in hand I enrolled by phone in a course of six one-hour lessons to see if I could pick it up.

The night before my first lesson I found I was actually quite nervous. I'd been wearing my tap shoes around the flat to get the feel of them, but I had wooden floors at the time and the woman downstairs kept banging on the ceiling with a broom because of the noise. On top of that, when I went to bed, I had a dream that I'd got an audition for a Hollywood movie and had to perform a very complicated tap routine with Gene Kelly. Of course it all went horribly wrong and I got evicted from the studio in disgrace.

The next day I took a bus the few stops to my first lesson. En route we passed a large tavern. Outside in the street was a very drunk elderly man with a long trench coat and trilby hat having a bash at his own very wobbly Fred Astaire dance routine to an imaginary audience. I thought to myself, that'll probably be me a couple of hours from now if these lessons don't go well.

In the school's entrance lobby, there was a large green baize pin board advertising all the different things you could learn. There was Singing for Beginners, Acting with Shakespeare, Spiritualism in the Twenty First Century, Learn Ancient Chinese, Yoga and Relaxation, and the Dying (if not already dead) Art of Macramé. Also, apparently, on a Thursday night was Expressive Cake Baking in the extensive modern, recently upgraded kitchen in the cellar. Then I found Tap Dancing with Mavis Cankerwood, fifth floor. I looked at my watch and I was already nearly ten minutes late. Looking around I could see there was no lift. Perhaps five flights of stairs was the keep fit bit spoken of in the ad?

By the time I reached the fourth floor I was beginning to get a little puffed out, but the sound of tap dancing from above drew me on. On the studio door was a sign in big letters saying, "Lesson in progress, please knock before entering." I knocked but they didn't notice me. I realised I would have to knock out of time with the dancing, which as silly as it may sound was surprisingly difficult to do – a bit like rubbing your stomach and hitting the top of your head at the same time. I took one of my tap shoes from my bag and hammered it loudly against the wood. The tap dancing from inside stopped. After a moment or two I opened the door a crack and peeked inside. The room was empty. I was a bit baffled as I had just stood outside and heard a lively routine in progress... not a particularly good routine mind, though I was not in a position to criticise just yet. Perhaps I'd got the day wrong and instead happened upon Spiritualism in the Twenty First Century, the ghosts of tap dancers passed.

I began heading back down the stairs disappointed. I thought at worst I could keep going to the cellar and wait until someone baked me an expressive cake. But when I reached the third floor, the tap routine upstairs began again. I ran back up and straight into the room. There was a tall thin anxious looking woman at the front of a wood blocked area surrounded by carpet. With her were three students - a short fat girl, a spotty teenage boy and a tall willowy blonde creature in full purple Lycra dance togs. They all jarred with fear as I entered.

'Can I help you?' said the thin woman.

'I'm here for the lesson, I'm sorry I'm a bit late,' I answered.

'Are you Jeff?' she said, walking towards me with a hand outstretched. I nodded. 'I'm Mavis Cankerwood. Was it you who knocked just now?' I nodded again. 'I'm so sorry we thought you were mad Sophie. She's so disruptive to the class and never brings her fee. I've tried so hard to stop her coming but she never takes the hint. So now we just hide and she usually goes away again.'

Just then we could hear a voice from the stairs outside. 'Hello? Hello?' Mavis jumped.

'It's her, quick!' She grabbed my arm and we all ran across the carpet and into a cupboard. Forty minutes we stood there in the dark waiting for mad Sophie to leave.

'I'm so sorry you've missed your lesson,' said Mavis afterwards. 'Better luck next week, perhaps?'

Two days later Mavis phoned to say she was moving her class to the other side of town. I gave my tap shoes to a friend. To show their gratitude they bought me a big bunch of flowers. And a very expressive cake.

MERINGUE AND SEAMEN

It was third time lucky for the taxi. We'd been along The Embankment on the River Thames twice already, but locating a specific boat with no address or postcode was far more than even a cab driver's Satellite Navigation could cope with. For the life of us, we just couldn't find a vessel called The Maureen. After a quick phone call to re-advise that we should instead be looking for "the mooring," we finally discovered where I was supposed to be.

I'd never done a show on a boat before. In the week leading up to it, I'd imagined it to be quite exotic and perhaps a little glamorous. My imagination promised a life on the ocean waves with lots of fit young crewmen frigging-in-the-rigging, groping-in-the-roping and using the planking for things we can only dream about. Don't even get me started on how many different types of Seamen there are. But as per usual in my job, the anticipation was far more interesting than the reality ever could be.

'I'm sticking you in here,' said Desmond, holding his guest-list clipboard between his teeth to pull open a distant cupboard door with both hands. 'It's got a mirror and a sink because it used to be a toilet, but we closed it off because it's faulty. So I will warn you, no solids down the pan otherwise it may back up again. And effluence is a bugger to pick out from the grooves between the decking planks.' He screwed up his pinched face at the memory. 'You might like to leave this door ajar for a bit, give it an airing. It's not been used for two years.' I glanced inside.

'The floor seems damp considering it's not been used,' I observed. 'Have you got a mop?'

'Tell you what, I'll get you some newspaper to put down,' he said, tapping his white-gloved hand on my arm. I attempted to open the door wider, but it was jammed against the floor.

'It's a nice evening, I could leave the door open,' I offered. 'Will my stuff be safe at this end of the boat?' He raised his eyebrows and tilted back his head like Pat Phoenix, looking at me disapprovingly across the top of his spectacles.

'This is not a boat, this is a yacht!' he snapped, before turning on his heels and gliding back to the gangplank to greet a further cluster of revellers.

Despite the bad start, I did get a wink from one of the sailors as he pulled in the ropes and the boat… sorry… the yacht slowly pulled away from the dock. As the natural light through my open door began to dim, I realised it wasn't going to be easy finishing my makeup. The toilet light bulb was not really adequate, so I had to take a hand-mirror outside where the deck lights were much brighter. Thankfully, the party was taking place at the front end so I was left alone, which was just as well as I had to redo my eyebrows three times. Every time I got to the crucial arch of the brow, a wave tipped us and my eye-pencil shot up my forehead. I was beginning my show with an impersonation of Diana Ross. Standing at the handrail watching the sights of London drift slowly by, I could see lots of people waving and taking photos from the shore. From a distance, they perhaps thought I was the real thing. I waved back regally, not wishing to disappoint.

Suddenly, Desmond arrived. 'We're running about an hour-and-a-half late in the kitchen, you'll have to wait. We've only just taken out the main course then they've got the Meringue Surprise to get their teeth into. And it will be one hell of a surprise if it still hasn't de-frosted.' The novelty of sight-seeing had already worn off by this time.

'Can I wait inside, it's getting quite breezy now,' I asked hopefully.

'Well, I can put you a chair at the end of the front table of the dining hall, but you'll be sitting with the diners.'

'Can't I wait in the kitchen? I don't want them to see me in costume before the show starts,' I said.

'It's not a kitchen, it's a galley,' he frowned, throwing his head back again, 'and I wouldn't advise it, they're in tears down there, they're frantic. It's the damned meringue, you see,' he sighed, looking at his watch before marching decidedly back towards the hall.

I finally started my show two hours behind schedule. My audience weren't too happy from the start, though they did warm to me as my performance progressed. I don't know about the meringue, but I didn't de-frost until about three songs in. One broad woman sitting near the front spent most of the first ten minutes discovering yet further bits of crumbled meringue in the folds of her frock's ruffled neckline. Disaster struck when I did my Kate Bush tribute. Mid-routine up on one foot with my left leg in the air, the yacht dipped in the wake of a larger passing vessel. I lost my balance and shot across the surface of one of the tables, knocking everyone's drinks into their laps. My big red crimped wig got caught on a woman's earring. It ripped from my shaven head as I stood back up, which raised a laugh and saved the show, though not my dignity.

A downside of performing at sea that I hadn't anticipated was that I couldn't leave once the show had finished. Instead I had to wait a further three hours until we docked. But it was an experience I will never forget. And I did go home with a big box of Meringue Surprise, which de-frosted just in time for supper.

TRAIN OF THOUGHT

By the time I'd queued to get my train ticket, I really needed to wee. Luckily I knew there was a toilet on my platform. Aside from a little fat boy scoffing a family sized bag of crisps I was the only one there, though there were quite a few people on the opposite platform. Alas, the loo was shut with a sign on the door which read, "Closed due to flooding. Please use the toilets at Frampton House."

'Where's Frampton House?' I asked the Station Master. It was about a quarter of a mile away and I wasn't sure I'd make it that far, having already held on for some time. And I couldn't bear the thought of using the convenience on the train. 'Can I have the key for the disabled toilet?' I asked hopefully.

'Suppose someone disabled wants to use it?' he growled disapprovingly. I looked up and down the platform. I was still alone other than the fat boy, who stopped chewing and snapped shut the top of his crisp bag when we looked at him, perhaps believing we had our eye on sharing his enormous snack.

'What about her?' said the Station Master, pointing opposite to an ancient lady propped up in a wheelchair.

'I'm not being funny,' I said, 'but by the time she's got up thirty steps across the bridge and back down this side I'd have finished. Her only alternative is to go out of the station around the block and come in this side and frankly she doesn't look like she'd survive the journey.' He thought for a moment. I could hear cogs whirring from inside his earhole.

'Have you got a disability card?' I shook my head. 'Alright, I'll get the key. But don't tell anyone.' Like who? I think he was walking slowly on purpose, as though allowing time for the possibility of a coach full of disabled people arriving suddenly and proving his point. Either that or he just wanted to emphasise the enormous effort he was putting in to help me. Either way, by the time he unlocked the door I was so desperate that my teeth were itching. But when my train arrived, I was suitably relieved.

I had decided upon a journey of quiet contemplation and thought. Snuggling into a left-hand chair in a little alcove of four, I took out some of my writing notes. I could feel the warmth from the sunshine against my face as we pulled gently from the station. Suddenly my attention was drawn to a strange high-pitched sound in the distance but getting louder. As we slowed into the next station it became apparent that the noise was a child screaming from the platform. It continued to screech like nails down a blackboard as it entered my carriage, along with its enormous bare-armed tattooed mother. They were followed closely by a matching woman dragging a snotty nosed boy of about six by the scruff of the neck.

'Get in here you little runt,' she screamed at him. At least, I think she said runt? He ran and jumped up onto the seat opposite me, bouncing up and down kicking the wall. The women ignored him as they hauled themselves into the adjacent alcove.

'Shut up!' yelled the tattooed mother at the screaming child. Too late, my ears were already bleeding. As the train pulled away, the boy leapt from his seat onto the one next to me.

'Oi, watcha reading?' he said, wiping the candle from his nose onto the next headrest while poking my shoulder.

'Words,' I replied in an attempt to show disdain. But it didn't work and suddenly I had the attention of the whole group.

'He's nosey ain't he, wanting to know what you're reading?' said the mother's friend. I nodded, trying not to get involved. 'Whatever it is you're reading?' she questioned. I still wasn't going to tell her. Out of the corner of my eye, I saw her look at the mother then back at me. I had now become a challenge. 'This train goes to London don't it?' she asked me. I nodded. 'I ain't never been to London. It's really big, ain't it?'

'You could say that,' I answered staring blankly at my notes. I was feeling penned in. Should I just get up and move to the next carriage? Or would that seem rude? But weren't they already being rude to me? But then, if they weren't aware of their own rudeness and actually thought they were being friendly to me, my leaving the carriage now would appear rude to them. Or should I just say I was going to the toilet but then actually go to the next carriage instead? And would they know I hadn't gone to the toilet but it wouldn't matter because by the time they'd realised, I'd already be gone? But what if there wasn't a toilet and they knew it? Then if I said I was going to the toilet they'd instantly know I wasn't. And should I even discuss going to the toilet with total strangers? I was drowning in my own Englishness! Only twenty minutes before I had been adamant I would not use a toilet on a train and now there I was longing for one. How could I get away from these horrible people? I needed a different approach.

'You work in London then?' they asked.

'Yes.'

'What do you do?'

'I'm a drag queen!' I replied with a wry smile. For the next ten minutes we travelled in blissful silence. And at the next station, they were gone.

DONNY, ZOE AND OLLY

'I've made up my mind and that's all there is to it,' said Zoe, taking a bite from her Victoria Sponge before lighting another cigarette. She had always been stubborn and generally, if ever she'd made up her mind to do something, she'd gone ahead and done it. Though I wasn't trying to talk her out of becoming a Mormon, I just considered it to be a big decision and wanted her to be sure she was making the right choice.

Zoe was a girl who loved a fad. I think deep down it was a yearning to be more interesting. She'd had a bash at every new trend or fashion over the fifteen years we'd known each other. She'd done the green hair and giant ring through the end of her nose like a pig for six months following The Prodigy. She'd done the tattoos and fluorescent punk for Pink and the blonde bunches and mid-rift for Britney. After putting on a little weight, she'd even done the big hair and eyelashes like Adele. But sitting in front of me now in her sensible Christian blouse, stuffing her face in the bright sunlight with no makeup and dark roots, sadly she just looked like Gemma Collins after three days in the I'm A Celebrity jungle. Her long-suffering parents were horrified that she wanted to be a Mormon. They were of the opinion that she would join a radical cult, grow horns and stop wearing knickers. I hadn't the heart to tell them she'd previously already done all of this just by following The Prodigy. But her announcement that she would be changing her name to Jean just made it sound like they would be losing their baby forever.

A week later I was sitting in the garden when the doorbell rang. Quite by coincidence, it was two Mormon men spreading their word. I invited them in for tea. Aside from the fact that they were both rather cute, I thought it may be a good idea to hear what Zoe... sorry, Jean was letting herself in for, if only to pacify her parents.
    'Thanks, but we don't drink tea or coffee because of the caffeine. We don't take any kind of drug that may poison our body because we see it as the temple that houses our soul,' said the brown-eyed baby with the American accent. I couldn't quite put my finger on who he reminded me of. Something about his face was familiar... But the principal of a drug-free existence sounded like good common sense to me. If it got Jean out of her forty-a-day fag habit, surely it can't be all bad? The other man was from The States, too. It took every ounce of self-control I could muster to not picture them sitting there dressed in a sexy baseball kit. Their names being Kirk and Brent just made them seem even more like porn stars, which didn't help. I managed to remain respectful under the circumstances and got an invite to their Church.

That Sunday as promised, the boys arrived to drive me to their gathering. This was the same Church that Jean would be joining. I'd explained that my visit was about supporting her and not about a personal conversion, but they were still happy for me to attend, as were the rest of their wonderfully friendly congregation. We entered a long corridor, which lead into a large high-ceilinged hall.

'I'm doing a baptism today, so I'll leave you with Kirk for a while,' said Brent.

'OK, bye for now. Be lucky,' I called after him, as he walked away up the passage.

'Do you notice anything different about our Church?' questioned Kirk.

'Yes, it doesn't have any crucifixes, does it?' I glanced about just in case I'd missed one.

'You're right, well done!' he smiled. 'If Jesus had been killed with a gun, we wouldn't have rifles hanging above the altar, either.'

'Isn't the crucifix there to remind people?' I asked.

'We don't need reminding,' he whispered, as everyone took a seat. I could see his logic. I looked around thinking we might sit with Jean, but she was nowhere to be seen. Suddenly, as the hall fell silent, a loud duck quacking rang out. Everyone looked around at their feet expectantly. I took my phone out of my pocket and apologised, explaining that the sound they had heard was my mobile telling me I had received a text. I switched it off and sank embarrassed into my seat. But I now had the giggles.

'Why are you laughing?' asked Kirk with a smile.

'I'm so sorry, I think it's just nerves,' I said, biting hard on my tongue. Then at the front of the hall, Brent walked out from a door to one side. He was dressed head to foot in baptism-white. In an instant, I realised who he had reminded me of… it was Donny Osmond! This just made me giggle more.

'Everyone says that,' apologised Kirk.

After the gathering, I walked home. The text had been from Jean… now once again known as plain old Zoe. Someone she knew had a spare Olly Murs concert ticket, so instead of coming to Church, she'd spent all afternoon shopping for a pork-pie hat, drainpipe trousers and waistcoat. Her parents were relieved. Perhaps it was for the best.

BACK WITH BERNIE

I was ironing my shirt when the text came. It was Aaron, the Best Man. "sorry. can you collect mrs hunt?" Though quite cute, Aaron was a bit of a meathead, so it was inevitable that something would go wrong with him organising transport for a wedding. It was no big deal for me, I was going alone so had a space in my car. After texting back my agreement, I received an address followed by a rather curious comment. "warning. it's hunt with a c, lol." I wasn't really sure what he meant.

Half an hour later, I was on the first floor of a small yellow-brick nineteen-sixties block. I tapped on the door and a small, wrinkled old lady answered. Dressed head to foot in a lavender two-piece with a cream beret and matching hand bag, she peered suspiciously up at me.

'Who are you?' she scowled, holding a hand up to shield her eyes from the bright sunlight.

'I'm Jeff, a friend of the groom. I've come to drop you at the wedding.'

'Which groom? I've got two weddings today, which one are you?' she grumbled.

'I'm Martin and Susanne,' I smiled.

'Oh dear.' She looked almost disappointed.

'Is something wrong?' I asked.

'I don't like her, I was hoping you was the other one.'

Back downstairs, she stopped as we approached my car. 'Is this it, then? Ain't you got no ribbon? There ought to be ribbon if we're going to a wedding. My husband Bernie would have had ribbon if he was still here.' I shrugged patiently and walked around to the driver's door as she climbed into her seat.

'You on your own?' she said, as we turned out of her Avenue. I nodded. 'What's the matter with you, then?' she added. I was beginning to understand why nobody else had wanted to collect her. We pulled up at a set of traffic lights in the busy high street.

'I'm not single, I'm just going to the wedding alone,' I said, turning to face her. But she was gone. The car door was open and she was walking across the pavement towards an old boarded-up shop. 'You can't get out here!' I called after her, but she was too distracted. I jumped from the car and ran to collect her.

'The Greengrocer's… look, it's all closed down! I used to like it in there.' As the lights changed green to go, the cars behind me started tooting their horns.

'Get back in the car, we're blocking the road,' I cried, taking her by the shoulders and pushing her back towards her seat.

'Can't you keep your mother under control?' yelled the driver behind. I walked around and climbed back in, clicking my seatbelt shut. I turned to face her again and she was jammed behind her seat with her elbow up on the parcel shelf at the back, one foot out of the window.

'What are you doing, Mrs Hunt?'

'I want to sit in the back,' she mumbled. I jumped out again and ran back round to her side.

'There isn't a back, it's a two-seater!' I said, helping her from the tiny crawl space. By the time we were back in position, the building traffic behind me was frantic because the lights were once again red. 'Are you alright?' I asked. She seemed a bit winded. 'Take some deep breaths,' I suggested as the green light re-appeared.

'I've lost my shoe,' she gasped, lifting her bare-toed foot into the air as I pulled away. 'I think it went out of the window!' The car bumped as we drove over it. I pulled up further along where the angry traffic could pass me more easily and ran back to collect her now mangled footwear. 'We'll have to go back home now, I can't go with one shoe,' she said, poking her finger through the hole where the heel had been.

We arrived at the wedding reception somewhat later than expected but fully heeled, with a spare pair she'd insisted on bringing along in case the same thing happened again. In the large hall full of over a hundred people, she was all but ignored. I actually felt quite sorry for her, so after saying my personal congratulations to the bride and groom, I got her another Sherry and sat beside her.

'If my Brian was here, they'd at least have said hello,' she said sadly. I thought for a moment.

'Didn't you say your husband's name was Bernie?'

'Yes, that's right, did you know him?' She smiled at me as her face lit up, the first time all day that I had seen her without a frown.

'Unfortunately no, but who's Brian?' I asked.

'I don't know,' she said, her frown returning.

'Do you still want to go to the other wedding?' I said.

'What other wedding?' she replied quietly. Hmm. Back in the car, I began to realise that she wasn't the grumpy old lady everyone wanted to avoid. In reality, she had lost her husband and then lost the plot, which made it difficult for anyone to relate to her, including her so-called family.

'I wish I'd met Bernie. Tell me about him, what was he like?' Her face lit up once more as she began her story.

Back at her flat, we sat for three hours with several cups of tea and half a dozen photo albums. She grasped my hand affectionately with a smile as I left. I heard a few weeks back that she had died. I wasn't sad for her. She is at last back with Bernie, where she belongs.

PICKLED PASSENGERS

'Isn't there any air conditioning on this train?' I asked the ticket inspector.

'Sorry sir, there is but it doesn't appear to be working. You'll have to make do with all the open air-vents,' he replied, further loosening his tie. No discount on my fare, then? To try to distract from the stifling heat, I decided to listen to some music on my mobile phone. As I put in my earpieces, I glanced around the train at the dozen or so other passengers in my carriage. All were suffering from one degree or another of slow cooking. A tubby man just across from me was bright red in the face and very restless. He had removed as much clothing as was decent and was wiping his brow with a sodden handkerchief. A thin mousey woman further up the aisle was fanning her face with a magazine. I closed my eyes and listened to the familiar melody in my ears, trying to ignore the sweat running down my sticky torso inside my shirt.

As I took a deeper breath of what little oxygen there was, I heard something over my music. It sounded like a scream. I opened my eyes to see chaos at the other end of the carriage. A tall man and a girl dressed as a Goth were on their feet and flapping their arms in the air as though trying to escape the heat by flying. When they grabbed their bags and ran in my direction, I realised there was something far more sinister going on.

'WAASSSSP!!' shouted the Goth girl all the way down the central aisle. The vengeful insect clearly didn't want to be left alone, following them and settling on destroying the dignity of the thin mousey woman. She leapt to her feet screaming, throwing her arms into a spasm around her head and hair, eyes darting fervently as though suddenly possessed by demons. She stood on her chair and bounced up and down a few times before running up the aisle past me to join the other victims. Another three passengers leapt into the crazy wasp dance as it passed through their personal space before finally reaching the tubby man. His eyes bulged with horror as it hovered in front of his face as if about to bite his nose. Without averting his stare, he grappled in his bag and pulled out a half-eaten pasty. The wasp followed his gaze as he rose to his feet, waiving the snack in front of the creature a few times before throwing it out of the slim vent at the top of the window. Unfortunately, the wasp didn't take the scent and follow, so he too ran to the top end of the carriage.

I suddenly found myself face to face with the nemesis. It hovered inches in front of me, teeth glistening in the bright sunlight, trying to stare me into submission. Time appeared to slow down as it shot vertically into the air and a rolled-up newspaper came crashing onto my headrest, missing my ear by a centimetre. I jumped from my seat in shock, narrowly missing a second swipe from a grey-suited alpha-male.

'You can't kill it!' I cried.

'Why not?' he growled, convulsing in an attempt to keep it in his sights.

'Because it's got as much right to be here as we have,' I said, grabbing my bag from the seat.

'Bollocks!' he spat, re-rolling the paper. 'It didn't pay twenty-five pounds for a ticket, so it's gonna die!'

The creature appeared to relish the competition, buzzing in circles around the alpha-male's head as he stood legs apart, swathing his weapon in the air with two hands like a lightsaber. Darting further up the aisle, I turned back to watch. From a distance, his Arthurian fight-to-the-death look quite ludicrous. Bored with his opponent, the wasp suddenly headed in our direction.

'Quick, into the next cabin,' panicked the thin woman.

'We can't, it's First Class,' gasped the tubby man. Someone pressed the hydraulic door button and ran into the sealed lobby between the two carriages. About eight people followed his lead. As the door shut behind them, they all turned and peered sheepishly back through the glass. I couldn't help but smile to myself. It looked like a jar of pickled passengers, all pressed up against each other, sweating and panting.

It was then that I noticed an elderly lady to one side, still sitting in her seat as the wasp darted about her hat. Calmly, she took a boiled sweet from her mouth and stuck it to the inside of the window. Leaving her hat, the insect settled on the sweet. The alpha-male paused in his vendetta and watched in frustrated wonderment.

'He's hungry, poor little devil!' said the old woman, picking up an empty paper coffee cup and upturning it over the banquet. She slid her People's Friend under the cup to hold the contents within, then without fuss, threw the cup and its inhabitant out the window. I looked back at the jar of pickled, dumbfounded and rather embarrassed passengers. As the door hissed back open, they hurriedly returned to their seats, comforted by renewed anonymity.

'Well done,' I said to the old lady, 'and thank you.'

'We were probably passing through his home,' she said with a knowledgeable smile. I think perhaps she was right.

FIREMAN FUND

I was met at the gate by a tall, thin security guard with a patch over one eye. 'So who are you?' he asked, quite understandably. I wondered if a man whose job it was to watch would only get half pay if he could only use one eye. But then it was a charity event.

'I'm here to perform,' I advised.

'Well, I don't recognise you from the poster. I took off my hat and sunglasses. 'Nope, still don't!' I pointed to my photo. 'Ah, you're the drag queen! Well why didn't you say so? In your dark glasses you looked like that singer... oh, what's his name? Sounds like a dog biscuit.' I thought for a moment.

'Bono?'

'That's the fellah. From that Duran Duran. "Please please tell me now!"' he sang. I smiled politely and entered through the gate.

I was due to sing at a festival to raise funds for injured Firemen in Essex. I had considered cancelling, but I'd been advertised and it was such a beautiful afternoon for an open-air gig. I wasn't really sure why my booker Denise had wanted a drag queen until I took a glance from backstage at the audience, which consisted mostly of drunken women.

'It's gonna be mad!' grinned Denise, taking a swig from a bottle of brightly coloured alco-pop. 'Three of the turns ain't come, so I'm glad you're here. Linda Maylem was going to sing. Do you know her?' I shook my head. 'She was gonna come but she got bit by a dog.'

'Where?' I asked, as she led me through to a large white tent.

'Camber Sands,' she replied. 'Is this alright for you?' She pulled back the tent flap to reveal a large carpeted area with several tables and chairs and a rail. To one corner were a collection of bags and some scattered clothes, which I assumed belonged to whoever was at that moment having a bash at "I'm Too Sexy" up on the stage.

'Lovely,' I smiled.

'Do you want anything to eat?' she asked. 'There's tons of sandwiches and some lime jelly.'

'No thanks, I've already eaten,' I said, glancing discreetly at the dirt under her fingernails.

'I was gonna make some apple crumble but the topping fell off when I turned it upside down to read the cooking instructions. I'll leave you to get ready then,' she said, exiting the flap.

In full costume, I adjusted my wig in the small dressing table mirror I had brought with me. I don't really like tempting fate by taking one in my suitcase, but experience has taught me that events like this often forget to install one in the dressing room. I smiled at the irony of the performers' closing song as they ran back into the tent.

'Hello, I'm Nishka,' smiled the female of the three Goths. 'This is Toulouse and this is Black.' She pointed at her two depressed looking companions.

'I'm Jeff,' I smiled with a wave across. 'I liked your final song, Relight My Fire. Very funny.' They stared back at me blankly. 'Relight My Fire? Fundraiser for firemen?' I explained.

'Oh yeah,' said Nishka, 'I never thought of that!' I turned sharply back at my mirror desperately trying to not to giggle.

My performance went well. I could be wrong, but I sensed the audience relax, knowing what to expect from a drag queen. Someone at the front shouted, 'Been a pile of shite so far, mate!' Thankfully the stage was quite high, as the crowd were quite rowdy and worse for drink. Though I did feel safer knowing I was now somebody's "mate."

The highlight of my performance was three uniformed firemen pushing through to the front and baring their chiselled chests at me. Well, at least they were dressed as firemen. I couldn't say for sure whether or not they were the real thing, but the gesture was appreciated. Mid song, I noticed from the corner of one eye that Denise was waving frantically at me from the wings. She was in full view of the audience, she may as well have just walked up to me.

'What?!' I quizzed comically, much to the delight of the rabble.

'Don't forget you've got to call the raffle,' she whispered as loudly as she could.

'How can I forget something you haven't told me about yet?' I shouted back. Returning to my song, I wondered how we would call a raffle in a field full of two thousand people. If someone at the back had the winning ticket, it would take them twenty minutes to push to the front and collect their prize!

Show over, I returned to the tent to remove my costume and makeup. Denise was nowhere to be seen, so I didn't hang around. Thankfully being a charity show, I didn't have to collect any money. I returned to the front gate.

'I heard you singing. You were quite good,' said the security guard.

'Why are you wearing an eye-patch?' I asked.

'I was driving along picking my nose and I went over a pot hole.' Ask a stupid question…

As I pulled out behind a long and painfully slow queue onto the motorway a few minutes later, I began to wonder why I had bothered going. But then a mile further up the road, the reason for the heavy traffic became apparent. A fire crew had just cut a woman from a smashed-up car.

COFFEE WITH CARMINE

My first encounter with my neighbour Carmine occurred on the stairway at our block of flats. The relationship didn't get off to a good start. She had a habit of clearing the back of her throat with a strange reverberating sound, a bit like a bear grunting. Standing with her hand to her throat on the mid-landing, I thought she was choking. I swiftly dropped my shopping bags and smacked her hard on the back. She lunged forward and banged her head on the wall, which didn't go down too well until I explained myself. Realising my intentions were good, she apologised for punching me back and invited me for coffee the next morning.

Her apartment was across the hall and an exact mirror image of mine. It was odd walking through the front door and turning left rather than right into the kitchen. It also seemed much smaller than mine, possibly because of the extraordinary clutter and huge flowered wallpaper adorning every wall. There was also a noxious smell, which she explained as a mixture of last night's Caribbean supper and bed linen boiling in an old-fashioned top loader washing machine. After showing me around her equally flowery bathroom and bedroom, we sat at a small table in the lounge as she poured hot water on our Mellow Birds.

'I've been here eight years since I left my husband,' she said, reaching across to stir my cup. 'He was very abusive and I found I had just had enough.'

'My God, that's terrible,' I replied, spinning my cup in my hand to avoid a large dark brown chip in the rim as I took a sip.

'Yes, he used to beat me.' I'd kind of expected us to be talking about something a little lighter so soon into our first proper conversation. I was a little uncomfortable and not too sure what to say. As she took a sip, I noticed that both her eyes looked in a different direction. It was hard to tell if she was talking to me or someone who'd just walked into the room behind. 'Before we married, he used to be my neighbour,' she continued, squinting suspiciously. I shifted awkwardly in my chair. 'When I was a young girl living at home, he used to follow me to the children's playground every Thursday and hang his hose over the fence.' I spat my coffee back into my cup with shock.

'Why did he do that?'

'Thursday was his day off.'

'His hose?' I questioned. She nodded, pointing one eye to her crotch by way of explanation. 'Oh, you mean his penis?'

'Yes,' she squealed. 'Dutty, dutty man he was. Enormous big black thing, wiggling about.'

'Didn't you report him?' I asked.

'I was going to, but after two years he stopped.'

'Why?'

'The Council put metal spikes on the fence.' As awful as this story was, I was trying not to laugh, thinking of the gay men I know who would give their right arm for such a neighbour.

'And yet you still married him?' She thought for a moment before answering.

'Well, I felt as though I already knew him intimately.' I didn't ask her to elaborate.

It was with some apprehension that I returned the favour by asking her to visit me for coffee the following week. I'd spent all morning cleaning, polishing and dusting to set a good impression. She arrived twenty minutes late and handed me her own mug as she walked into the hall. Clutching her handbag to her chest, she walked straight through to the lounge while looking around and grunting. I wasn't sure whether they were grunts of despair or approval or she was just clearing her throat again, as I signalled to the table and chairs for her to sit.

'It's very pink,' she said, as I poured.

'I find it a very calming colour,' I defended, offering a rich tea biscuit. She took two and placed them on the table next to her cup. 'And it's brighter. You catch the afternoon sun on this side.'

She stared at me intently, as though waiting for me to begin by telling her about my sexual past. I found myself trying to think of something equally profound, but nothing would come to mind. 'Where is your toilet?' she asked. I was relieved for the distraction, though it was a rather strange thing to ask.

'In the same place as yours.' She nodded, and with another grunt, stood from her chair and disappeared into the inner hall. I sat for a moment, contemplating how silly this whole coffee meeting was. I hardly knew the woman, and though having coffee was perhaps a good way to get to know someone, I wasn't really sure I wanted to know Carmine. Suddenly there came a shriek. I ran to see what was wrong. But she wasn't in my bathroom, she was in my bedroom at my open wardrobe, holding aloft one of my drag costumes.

'You have a very glamorous wife,' she said with a laugh.

'Ah... actually they're mine.' Her smile turned instantly into a frown.

'You didn't tell me you was a chi chi man!' she growled disapprovingly.

'A what?' I asked. She threw the costume on the bed and stormed from the room.

'Batty, batty, batty,' she murmured as I followed her back into the lounge. Snatching her cup from the table, she turned to face me as if for an explanation, but I couldn't be bothered. With a final grunt of disapproval, she headed for the front door and was gone.

GERRY'S UDDERS

'Nobody said anything to me about armpits! Why don't they warn you about these things before you leave home?' Gerry wasn't happy.

'Why, what's the problem?' I asked her.

'I haven't shaved. Can you try and get me a razor? I can't go in case they call me in. And don't tell anyone.' I wasn't sure how easy it would be to find a razor in a hospital without asking. Gerry had found a lump in her breast, and though the doctor had confirmed it as a harmless cyst, he had rightly sent her for an ultrasound to double check. According to the counter clerk, they would be checking her armpits at the same time. I looked around the waiting room full of women staring sympathetically at Gerry flapping. I headed out into the warren of corridors to see what I could find.

'There's a nice little shop next to the discharge lounge,' offered one helpful woman. I followed her directions and entered the shop, unable to wipe from my mind the gruesome thought of every kind of medical discharge occurring in the room next door. I managed to get Gerry a disposable razor, and she disappeared into the toilet for fifteen minutes to attend to her unsightly pits. I had to tap on the door to tell her we were being moved to another waiting area. As soon as she re-joined me, we were once again re-located.

'Moving us from one seating area to another like this is just a ploy to make you believe you're not being ignored,' she moaned, adding to the air of anticipation and fear in this even busier seating group.

'It's like cattle,' I offered. 'They're just shifting everyone to the appropriate pen.'

'Are you comparing me to a cow?' she snapped. 'I'm not here to get my udders seen to!'

'When did you find this lump,' I asked, delicately changing the subject.

'It wasn't me who found it, it was Jake. Or was it Arron? I can't remember now.' She took a small compact from her handbag and checked her face for shine. 'I've not been able to watch Corrie all week because it's got the same storyline.'

At that moment, a shocked lull fell over the waiting area, as a woman walked out of one of the adjoining rooms in floods of tears. But there was a collective sigh of relief when we realised she was actually crying with laughter at a joke one of the nurses had told her. A small round of applause broke out, which was strangely quite poignant. Suddenly, the woman sitting next to Gerry dropped her takeaway coffee on the floor. It bounced, as the plastic lid sprung open and splashed the dark brown liquid up the front of Gerry's beige trousers and matching suede shoes. Horrified, the woman ran to the toilet, returning moments later with half a toilet roll to wipe the floor and dab Gerry's legs.

'Oh, God!' Gerry cringed. 'As if it's not humiliating enough having to get my tits out for this scan in front of a complete stranger.'

'Don't talk daft,' I said. 'Half the men in London have seen your tits. Anyway, if you hadn't had your legs crossed for a change, the coffee splashes would just look like a tie-dye design. You won't be able to send them back to the catalogue now.' My attempt to lighten her mood had failed.

She turned to me with daggers in her eyes, shouting, 'It's alright for you drag queens, you can take your tits off when you've finished with them, we have to carry them around with us all the time!' Suddenly realising how loudly she had said this, she covered her face with her hand and sank back into her seat. The other women all looked me up and down, no doubt trying to imagine me dressed as one of them. I smiled warmly, mindful of how stressed they all must be. Though one or two did seem grateful of the distraction. The two nurses in the adjoining corridor had seen this. One of them approached.

'Oh, she's coming over! She's going to throw us out,' squirmed Gerry.

'Don't be silly, of course she won't throw you out.'

'It's Miss Colden, isn't it?' asked the nurse. Gerry nodded. 'We're running a bit behind schedule. Perhaps if you wouldn't mind, you could get your breasts out now to save time when we take you in?' Gerry was mortified, as were several of the other women. Then the nurse laughed. 'Ha ha! Just my little joke to make you smile and lighten the gloom. I'm like that aren't I, Sue?' she gestured back to her colleague. The other nurse nodded, raising her eyes to the ceiling with mock disgust. As the hospital's answer to Jo Brand walked away giggling, I took Gerry's hand and squeezed it supportively.

'Thank you for coming,' she said, with a smile. Twenty minutes later, a tall thin nurse came to collect her for her scan. As they walked away together up the corridor, I heard her say to Gerry, 'I love your trousers. Are they designer? People don't usually dress up to come for NHS. And you got the shoes to match so well, where did you buy them?' Gerry shot me a knowing glance over her shoulder.

Thankfully, her scan confirmed there and then that it was indeed just a harmless cyst. I can only pray that the other comrades in our waiting area were as fortunate in their results.

CHILDREN OF THE MASTER

Philip sounded unsure. 'To be honest, it's a bit of an odd one.'

'Odd? How do you mean?' I asked. I'd known my agent for some years, and it was unusual for him to be unsure of anything.

'They're nice enough people, just a bit... weird. You're the second one I've tried to get in there.'

It was with this in mind that my driver Thomas and I set off one Sunday evening for a church hall in South London. I was to perform in drag (of a sort) impersonating Cliff Richard for the seventieth birthday of someone's mother. As Thomas' elderly mum Annie was also a Cliff fan, we collected her on the way.

'Will I have to pay to get in?' she asked.

'Certainly not, you're coming as my guest,' I explained. As we pulled onto the venue's long tree-lined drive, it became clear that this was no ordinary church hall. Newly built and adorned with white Grecian pillars to either side of the entrance, it looked more like a funeral home. Established flowering shrubbery lined a path to the austere wooden doors, shielded from the late summer sunshine by an immense triangular portico adorned with a golden sunburst. We were greeted in the car park by a smartly suited man. 'Hello, I'm Jeff the cabaret,' I said, winding down my window.

'Greetings, I'm Adonijah. Welcome to our Church.' Thomas started giggling.

'Where should I park?' I asked.

'Are you children of The Master?' said Adonijah with a smile.

'If I'd have known he was here, I'd have brought my harness and gimp mask!' Thomas whispered.

'No, I don't think we are, are we?' I replied, turning for a response from inside the car.

'Then you'd better park around the back,' he said, pointing to a road up the side of the building. This just made Thomas giggle even more.

'I don't know what he's talking about,' moaned Annie. 'I was born Catholic, I didn't expect to be sent round the tradesman's entrance.'

A short, sweaty looking middle-aged woman in a flowery nineteen fifties Sandra Dee dress skipped (yes, skipped!) to us from the back door. 'You must be Cliff!' she gushed, shaking my hand. 'I'm Myrtle, welcome to our Church.' She led us into a squeaky-clean fluorescent lit corridor. 'I'm going to put you in the men's toilet, I hope that's OK? Nobody else will be using it.'

'Pity,' quipped Thomas. She looked shocked as Annie followed us in.

'You can't go in there!' she cried.

'It's OK if she does, as it's just a dressing room,' I smiled. 'You can come too, if you like?' She poked her head inside the door.

'Oh my word, what's that?' she said, pointing.

'It's a urinal.'

'Gosh, can I bring the others to see?' She skipped off up the corridor to fetch reinforcements as I began to unpack my costume.

'Have we stepped into the Twilight Zone?' Thomas bitched. Moments later, Myrtle returned with Judy Garland and Doris Day.

'Did I say it's fancy dress?' she said, looking Thomas and Annie up and down disappointedly. 'Oh, and there's no smoking or drinking,' she added, as Annie took a pre-smoking-ban fag packet from her handbag. 'Can you take your bag out to the car if it has those in it?' Annie frowned.

'Well, can I at least get a cup of tea?'

'Oh, no,' said Doris. 'Tea has caffeine, it's a drug. But we've got some orange squash and biscuits! They ran from the room giggling.

'Fine firkin party this is gonna be!' whinged Annie.

'Do they not see the irony?' added Thomas. 'No fags, booze or drugs and she's dressed as Judy Garland?'

The hall had half a dozen Cliff posters Blu Tacked to the walls and decorative drapes of different coloured toilet rolls hung from the ceiling. During the sound check on stage, we were asked to stop and join everyone in prayer. 'Good luck with that, I'm going for a fag,' said Thomas, deserting me to join his mother in the car. My show was to be a surprise for the birthday girl. We had arranged for me to leap from behind a curtain singing "Congratulations". I dived from the wings to be faced by Roy Orbison pushing a small wrinkled Dusty Springfield in a tinsel-adorned wheelchair. It took them my first three songs to get her back down the stairs from the front of the stage. My audience was made up of about thirty unnaturally buoyant costumed men and women dancing in the middle of the floor. There was a Lulu, about ten Elvis's and a Dusty that could walk. At tables around the edges sat a further ten or so people with very bemused looks on their faces. I figured they were perhaps well-wishing friends who didn't belong to the church and were in as much shock as we were. I looked to the back of the stage at the DJ for support.

'I've done a few of these mate, they get easier,' he smiled optimistically. 'Last time they booked a Diana Ross. She refused to do it without a drink and went home.'

The show itself went well. Back in the dressing room I found a half-empty caffeine-laden Coke can, tucked away behind one of the loos. Perhaps Judy wasn't as ironic as we'd thought!

COAT OF MANY RUBBERS

'This is your dressing room,' said the rather dishevelled porter nervously, opening a door to the left. The empty room was as large as a tennis court. 'It's one of the function halls,' he said apologetically. 'We've set everything up for you, as requested.' With a squint, I could just make out a small chair and table with a mirror, some quarter of a mile away in the distant corner.

'Why didn't they set it up over here near the door?' I asked.

'Err... I'm not really sure, I'll find out,' he bumbled, retrieving a small pad and pencil to take notes. A plump, thin-haired man in an emerald velvet jacket arrived.

'Hello, Jeff darling!' he gushed, whipping a scarlet silk hankie from his top pocket and wiping his hand before shaking. 'I'm Hillary. So glad you could be our guest of honour. These HIV charity dinner functions are always such a panic, but somehow we muddle through,' he laughed, nervously before turning to the porter. 'Gavin, tidy yourself up a bit!'

'I've got to move the table nearer the door,' he whinged. Hillary sighed with disapproval.

'He does that "just got out of bed" look so well! Now, we have a rather special frock for you tonight. It's made completely from condoms, which we thought appropriate.'

'Not used ones, I hope?' I smiled, but he was far too stressed to get the joke. We walked across to the table and there, hanging from a coat stand, was the dress. It was basically a floor-length silver tunic with hundreds of multi-coloured condoms stapled all over to create a rainbow flag.

An hour later and now in makeup, I was ready to try it on. But it was way too small to do up at the back and extraordinarily long at the front. 'I think this must only be a size eight,' I said. Hillary was in a panic. 'I tell you what,' I suggested, 'let's cut twelve inches from the bottom and pin a panel into the back. The condoms will hide the join.' Some scissors and two-dozen safety pins later, the problem was solved. I turned to look in the mirror. The costume made me look about eighteen stone! Hillary was close to tears by this time. 'OK, let's remove the condoms from the waist so they're just hanging above and below. That will accentuate the bust and the hips and give it some shape.'

Finally, we had something resembling style. But it had the strangest of smells. 'I'm not going to be sitting too close to anyone, am I?' I asked cautiously. 'They might think it's me!' I gave it a few squirts around my neck with perfume. A few seconds later there was a fizzing sound. The scented Johnnies appeared to be melting. Another five minutes with the scissors and we had now had a rather glorious plunging neckline.

'Let's go through before anything else goes wrong!' gasped Hillary, with another wipe from his hankie. I was becoming accustomed to the nauseating smell, but I hadn't anticipated how much noise it would make as I walked. It was like rubbing balloons together and putting my teeth on edge. 'Oh dear, these things often seem better in the planning!' Hillary apologised.

We entered the hall of mostly male, dinner-suited diners to rapturous applause. 'This is Aaron De Luchi who created your marvellous dress,' said Hillary, introducing me to a very austere looking man.

'It's a lovely creation, Aaron,' I offered.

'It's supposed to be a coat,' he snapped. 'You've got it on back-to-front. It's meant to be worn over your dress and open at the front, training out at the back. Like Joseph? The coat of many colours?' He wasn't happy. But it did explain what had gone wrong.

Sitting on the wooden chair at the top table wasn't easy in a rubber. I couldn't move in any direction without a strange squeaking noise that seemed to echo around the room. Eating dinner wasn't any easier. With such a pungent odour, everything seemed to taste of rubber. As a young waitress leaned over from behind me, the ceramic terrine she was holding pressed on my shoulder. The friction against the Latex jogged her balance and a small floret of cauliflower fell into the open top of one of the condoms hanging over my right breast. It made it look as though it was full of sperm. After several discreet but unsuccessful attempts to retrieve it with a set of silver sugar tongs, I told her not to worry and that if anyone asked, I'd just tell them it was a trophy.

Suddenly without any prior warning, I was introduced to make a speech. 'Don't do more than ten minutes,' whispered Hillary. Ten minutes about what? As I stood, the chair stuck to my garment. I managed to shake it loose as I walked to the podium.

'I'm honoured to be here,' I began. 'I've done a headcount, and by my reckoning there's about three condoms here for each of you. So form an orderly queue outside my dressing room and I'll be with you after we've all had pudding.' As I curtsied to laughter, the bottom hem of the frock fused to the hips and folded the entire creation in half, showing my knickers as I stood. We raised six thousand pounds that night. It was probably the most successful frock I've ever worn.

FIFTY WORDS FOR SNOW

Apparently, the Eskimo have fifty words for "snow." Over the years a few words of my own have evolved, though they're perhaps not repeatable in polite society. The white stuff itself is not the problem, I quite like that. Draped across the landscape sparkling and glistening, and that unique ability it has to absorb sound, creating an eerie quiet that reminds us of Christmas. The deeper, crisper and evener the better, as far as I'm concerned. It's what happens to our infrastructure after just a few inches of snow fall that I find frustrating. A few inches of anything else and I'm usually quite happy.

One particular afternoon, I awoke to the sound of chaos in the street outside. Peering through my curtain, I was surprised to see there had been an unexpected blizzard overnight. The road was already a sheet of ice and one of my neighbours was arguing with a man whose car had somehow mounted the pavement and knocked a big clump of rendering from his garden wall. I made myself a coffee and stood looking out at my back garden through the French windows. Several pigeons were rummaging around in the undergrowth, up to their gussets in snow trying to find something to eat. Our resident squirrel Kevin saw me and jumped from his favourite fence post down onto the lawn in anticipation. I broke up several pieces of bread as I often do and threw it into the middle of the glowing landscape. Other birds quickly arrived, including a small sparrow, doing his best with a giant piece of crust while buried up to his neck. I was pondering how difficult it must be for them to find food in this weather when I was suddenly distracted by a noise outside my front door. The postman had completely lost his balance on the ice and slid head first into the bushes. Grabbing him by the sleeve of his jacket, I lifted him back onto his feet.

'You wanna salt this path,' he scowled, thrusting an envelope into my hand. You'd think standing there in my dressing gown and slippers would indicate I had only just got up. My letter had "final demand" stamped across the front. If the postman hadn't already skidded off up the street, I'd have pushed him back into the bushes. Thankfully I had a cabaret show that evening, the fee from which would swiftly cover the cost of my overdue credit card bill. However, within the hour another blizzard had set in. By the time I was ready to leave for work, the car was engulfed. I got a warm glow of revenge using the offending credit card to scrape my windscreen clear, though my fingertips were frostbitten. Reversing off the drive was an adventure, as was gliding up the street to the main road, the narrow corridor of parked cars waiting to be taken out like score markers on a pinball machine. I was very disappointed to discover that the highway had no grit to prevent us all from slip sliding about like a pack of playful penguins. A light, sprightly waltz ringing out from my car radio added a comic soundtrack to proceedings. Clearly the sudden blizzards had caught the local authority by surprise… nothing new there, then! Discovering that the motorway was also unprepared was a comedy waltz too far. The snowfall attacked relentlessly as vehicles struggled to stay in lane and queues quickly began to stack up. I soon realised that I would have to cancel my show and attempt to get back home again. If I didn't appear on stage, I would not get paid - so much for my credit card bill. Added to this stress was the growing realisation that I may not actually get home at all. I cruised at a snail's pace past abandoned cars and people wandering around aimlessly with mobile phones pressed against their frozen ears.

Finally reaching my turn off to re-route home, I was confronted with a long, curved slide of ice with vehicles of all shapes and sizes careering in all directions. A portly woman in a bright red coat stood up to her knees in snow next to her stranded car, flapping her arms like a deranged robin as if trying to fly home. A car passed me on the ice backwards, like a terrifying Alton Towers ride. The remainder of my slow journey home was a horrifying experience. I was very relieved to finally pull onto my drive.

Putting on the kettle, my mind returned to the cancelled show. I needed a financial solution and couldn't think where to start. Feeling very sorry for myself, I switched on my garden lights and, still in my coat and hat, stood outside my back door with a coffee. Looking around, I remembered how difficult it had been for the wildlife to find food. By comparison, my cash-flow problem didn't really seem so bad. Perhaps I should just stop stressing and lighten up a little. I had, after all, got home safely. Looking up, I could see that the bow of the tree which draped over my shed had swung in an arc, backwards and forwards in the wind across its roof. Carved deeply in the snow before me was a big smile.

TIME TUNNEL

When we moved to Kent, we bought a seventeenth century house known as Wishing Well Cottage. Legend had it that it sat on the footprint of an earlier brick house and that the well used to be the water supply for the village. It was beautiful, but needed a lot of work, not least the creation of a couple of off-road parking spaces. Down came the front wall and a section of lawn was removed from the side garden in readiness.

A week later, I returned from a weekend of shows in Scarborough to discover a deep hole dug in the centre of the remaining lawn. This was for a soak-away to drain water from the new drive, my partner Charlie assured me. But in the hole about three feet down was the top of what seemed to be a brick-arched tunnel.

'It looks Elizabethan to me,' I advised, as though I knew what I was talking about. 'I've watched Discovery, I know what goes on.' Charlie scratched his head in despair.

'Don't get any ideas, the new lawn arrives tomorrow,' he warned. A small crowd of neighbours began to appear.

'Is it an Anderson Shelter?' mused one little old lady. 'Although, wasn't there supposed to be a tunnel from the old house to the church?'

By the time I'd made eight cups of tea, the vicar had arrived. Apparently somebody had phoned him, concerned about security at the vestry. Someone else suggested it could enter the graveyard through one of the concrete memorials. He didn't approve.

'Perhaps we should call Time Team,' he frowned.

'Yes,' I added. 'We can stick Tony Robinson in the back bedroom.' Charlie's grimace lightened to a smile because we had recently realised that the room was haunted.

'Tony won't have to guess who lived here by digging up a lump of brick and an old button, he could just ask the ghost.' The vicar didn't approve of this either.

'I don't know what all the fuss is about, it's probably just a drain,' said Charlie in a vain attempt to get the new neighbours off his land.

'No, can't be. The Elizabethans didn't have drains,' said the man from the bungalow opposite. 'They probably just tipped everything down the well.'

'Ooh, that's not very nice, it's drinking water,' said the old lady, as though I'd just made our tea by scooping from the bucket.

'Dig down a bit more,' said another man, taking Charlie's shovel and helping himself to our garden.

'You won't find anything,' said Charlie, lighting a cigarette.

'Maybe not,' came a puffed reply, 'but if this is a tunnel to the church, it must run under Daphne's house.' Charlie thought for a moment.

'Do you reckon that ghost of ours can use this tunnel to get into your cellar, Daphne?' he said. She frowned, grabbing at her pearls.

'I ought to go and check, I think I've got a crucifix,' she stuttered, heading off home. Charlie gave me a wink.

'One down,' he whispered before adding, 'I wonder if there's anything in the church records about a tunnel? There may be a clue about the other end.' That was the vicar's cue to leave. Charlie was on a roll. 'Of course, we could always put a door on the front of the arch and use it to store your drag queen dresses.' That got rid of another two.

As curiosity dwindled, the other man put down the shovel and went home for his tea. Finally alone, I asked Charlie, 'Aren't you just a little bit interested in where it might go?'

'No,' came the blunt reply. Twenty minutes later, the hole was filled with hardcore and topped with a layer of soil ready for tomorrow's turf delivery.

Digging began once more at dusk briefly when some woman's cat was reported missing, but the panic was over when they found him asleep on a grow bag in their shed. There was a lot of noise that night from the haunted bedroom. 'Perhaps you should have filled in the hole while the ghost was visiting Daphne's,' I smiled.

THE KILLING OF BERNARD

There was a stain on one of my patio slabs that looked like Bernard Cribbins. Or perhaps it was just a nondescript blob reminding me to read my script. Another day another casting, as they say, but I had already been headhunted for this new production. The problem was, nobody could really make up their mind which part would be played by whom. And it also hadn't yet been figured out whether The Killing Of Bernard By The Butler would be stage, cabaret or radio. So, into the breach I stepped, hoping today would be the day I could help everyone commit to a final decision. Easier said than done. My train was running late, the tube line I needed was closed for its monthly security scare and the substitute bus service reluctantly laid on by London Transport was still nowhere to be seen. Sitting at the temporary bus stop, I turned to page one of the script and dived in. The description by the author as "a period murder mystery set in the nineteen twenties" immediately rang alarm bells. If we know from the title that Bernard is killed by the butler, where is the mystery? And was the premise that "the butler did it" a double bluff or just bad writing? It's a luxury for any actor to be cast on their reputation, but I was mindful that even A-listers have had to audition for really good parts. With a loud screech and a rather worrying knocking noise, the standby bus finally pulled into the stop. I found a seat at the back and continued reading.

By the time I reached my destination, I had all but finished. Bernard and several others were indeed dead and the statement about what the butler did was merely an assertion by the real murderer to throw everyone off the scent. So far, so good. Or so I thought, until I entered the rehearsal room to find an argument in full swing. A tall skinny woman was trying to take a chair from a red-faced, grey-haired man who appeared to want to wrap it around the director's head. My sudden appearance thankfully distracted everyone as Grant, the director, ran to greet me.

'Thank God you're here,' he sort of smiled, loosening his tie. 'Everyone, this is Jeff,' he announced. Silence fell, as the assembled crowd looked me up and down like I'd been disappointingly booked as the cabaret stripper.

'You look smaller than you do on TV,' said a middle-aged man with a ginger beard.

'Well that's surprising, considering they say telly adds two stone to your weight,' I laughed, thinking I'd found a way to diffuse the obvious tension.

'I was referring to your height,' he replied cynically, glancing at my midriff.

'Shall we get started, then?' said Grant, with a cough. I was asked to read two parts, my quite possibly intended role of Detective Myers, and that of The Dowager Lady Belsham, which I plunged into with the best Maggie Smith I could muster. This role had actually been intended for old Mrs Cunningham apparently, but she had pulled from the production just two hours before on account of something to do with her kidneys. Whether she was cooking them or had a medical emergency was unclear, but I was advised that my occasional role as a professional drag queen made me the best qualified to take her place.

Despite earlier tensions, the reading actually went quite well. Gloria, the skinny woman with the chair, had to make Peter, the writer, a strong cup of tea at one point when he started to cry. Someone mentioned aside that it could be on account of his cat recently dying, but it transpired that he was just getting emotional to hear his written word come alive from the page. Upon the reading of the final line, everyone applauded vigorously. Peter started to cry again.

Then Grant turned to me, asking, 'So, what do you think?' Suddenly, everyone was silent again, hanging on for my detailed analysis as though I had the qualifications of Alan Bennett. I shot Grant a brief look of feigned gratitude.

'Let's all have a cup of tea and think about what just happened here,' I said, trying not to sound too drama school. Once we'd got the unnecessary mention of the butler in the title out of the way, everything else fell into place quite nicely. I was to play the dowager, as it was considered easier to re-cast the detective. Things got a little tetchy when I mentioned that, on stage or in cabaret, the maid being pushed down the stairs would be difficult to fulfill successfully without the risk of serious injury. So after a few more tears, Peter changed this to a hit over the back of the head with a wax Champagne bottle. I also delicately mentioned that, although Gloria's portrayal of Miss Merryweather being choked to death by the ramming of a carrot down her throat was inventive, on radio it may sound a bit like a blowjob. I quite liked the play and the role of the Dowager, but I never heard from any of them again. I'm not even sure if the production went ahead without me. Was it something I said?

ONE FOOT IN THE BATH

When I was young, we mostly used to wash in the kitchen sink, though my mother would regularly take me to the Bath House in Bermondsey for a once-all-over. I can still hear the often-raucous voices of the working-class cubicle occupiers echoing up the municipal corridors, "More hot water in number six!" So even now some considerable years later, I still think of a private bath in my own home as something of a luxury. I find lying in the tub especially relaxing before a long drive to work, but it's also good for my throat, breathing the steam, and practical for such things that are not as easy in a shower, like shaving my toes.

After several months of making do without a bath in my new home, the day had finally arrived for a brand new one to be installed. I had planned the afternoon to perfection. I'd bought lovely fluffy new towels and luxury French soap, and a cherry blossom bath bomb stood waiting expectantly on my bathroom windowsill especially for the occasion. The plumber would be finished by four, leaving about an hour to indulge before I had to take myself off to perform on stage in London. Everything was ready and utter bliss was on the agenda. I sat naked on the toilet seat watching with glee as the clean, sparkling water spilled into the oasis of calm. Anyone who had seen me would think I was mad getting so excited over water coming out of a tap. But I didn't care, in fact I was getting quite emotional by the time the bath bomb began to bounce and fizz. Ready for paradise, I plunged one foot in. At that very moment, there was a rather frantic knocking at my front door, followed by a petit Scottish drawl through my letter-box.

'Helloooo? Is there anybody there?' It was old Mrs Calcuddy from two doors down. I paused for a moment, trying to decide whether to answer of just pretend I wasn't in. 'I can see your light on… it's an emergency…' Reluctantly, I stepped back out, dabbing my foot dry on the floor towel and throwing on a dressing gown.

Since moving in, I had befriended the "Hebridean Hurricane", as the other neighbours liked to call her. Short and fiery, she always seemed keen to stop and talk and I'd often wondered if she wasn't perhaps a little lonely. Though usually I did have to bloody concentrate just to decipher her broad accent.

'What's up?' I asked, poking my head around my front door.

'There's a pussy on my roof,' she exclaimed excitedly. 'It's stuck. I know you like the wee monsters, so I thought I'd ask you to help to get rid of it.' I should just explain that she had previously mentioned she wasn't a fan of felines. In fact, I'd once had to persuade her not to lob a house brick at one innocently drinking from her pond.

'I just had one foot in the bath,' I complained, thinking she may suggest an alternative solution.

'When are you washing the other one?' she joked with a giggle. 'Oh well then,' she sighed, 'I'll get my garden rake out the shed.'

'No, don't do that!' I cried. 'Just give me a moment and I'll get dressed.'

As I looked up from outside her front gate, I could see the cutest, tiniest grey and white kitten in a small pink collar, sitting anxiously in the guttering along her bungalow roof. Mrs Calcuddy handed me a short stepladder. My first attempt immediately under the kitten failed miserably, as the foot of the ladder sank into the lawn and tipped me into a crevasse between a huge lavender bush and the front wall. Mrs Calcuddy laughed, as did another neighbour of ours who had come out to watch the mounting drama. Now caked in mud created by an earlier shower of rain, I pulled myself out from the shrubbery as it once again began to pour from the clouds. The pussy's plight had suddenly become more desperate, as indeed had mine. I reset the ladder on the front path thinking I'd have to climb on the roof, but thankfully the kitten ran along the gutter to meet me. Sodden and frightened, the poor little thing cried to me for help.

'Have you got a blanket or something I can wrap her in?' I asked.

'It must have shimmied up the drainpipe like a rat. Just catch it in a bin bag and throw it over next door's fence,' she cackled, handing me a clean fluffy tea towel.

'Ay, you've a wee wicked way with you, Mrs Calcuddy,' I smiled.

'You won't need to wash the other foot now, it's already wet,' she observed un-sympathetically.

By the time I had returned the poor sodden little baby to the address on her collar and got back indoors, I had little or no time left to languish in the bath. The cherry blossom powder from my bath bomb had sunk to the bottom, giving the appearance of a large colourful empty fish tank. As I put my foot back in, I realised that the water was now cold. I would just have to take a quick shower as usual. Feeling sorry for myself, I thought for a moment about the little kitten - warm and safe, snuggled up at home with her family. Suddenly, my self-indulgence didn't seem quite so important. My toes could for the moment remain hairy and my night of unbridled ecstasy in the bathroom could very easily wait until another day.

NO DANCING FOR FRED AND GINGER

Ginger was a person, not a cat. And I'm not really sure why his name was Ginger, it certainly didn't relate to his appearance. But rather delightfully, having recently lost five stone of his once considerable bulk, he now had a wonderful zest for living life to the full, which was lovely other than for the fact that everyone else had to get involved. As pleased as I was for him, there were indeed downsides to his immense weight loss. A tattoo of Robbie Williams on his right bicep now looked like Sid James, and with the zeal of a newly reformed non-smoker, he was now insistent that all his friends needed to dance to the same tune. Insert Fred Astaire joke here.

So it was, he had decided I was to accompany him on a day trip to France. He'd been several times recently with several people and now apparently it was my turn. I had been reluctant at first, but now the trip was imminent, I was actually quite looking forward to it.

'I know some fabulous places to shop, so we need to get lots of Euros before we go,' he gushed, briefly flashing the Chanel label on his new coat. It didn't look like a Chanel to me. While he was in the toilet, I had a closer look at the label. It was actually from the Channel Tunnel gift shop. What looked from a distance like the iconic inverted double-c Chanel logo was in fact the face of two tunnels. I smiled to myself. You had to admire his impiousness.

I hadn't really considered how much preparation would have to go into a day trip abroad. The first decision was how to get there. Other than lying on the beach and the odd paddle, I'm not a big fan of the sea. Should we float on top at the risk of sinking or falling in, or should we go underneath, perhaps on the very day that the tunnel would flood? Either way I would drown, so I opted for the quicker route by train. Ginger pointed out that with the Eurotunnel we could do Folkestone, Calais and then zip on to Paris, though this sounded more than a mere day's shopping to me. Either way, comfortable walking shoes were in order, and a rummage through the drinks cabinet to make a list for Duty-Free.

On the way back from picking up some Euros, I popped into the chemist for some travel sickness pills, where I was a little distracted by their canisters of oxygen - should I be forced to spend any amount of time under deep water. I also bought a new travel umbrella and some sucky-sweets for the journey.

Early one very cloudy and windy Friday morning, we met at St Pancras station to begin our quest. We had decided to give Folkestone a miss as it probably just had the same shops as Lewisham anyway, giving us time to do two locations in fashionable France. The journey wasn't as frightening as I thought it would be. I had taken a Barbara Taylor Bradford with me as a distraction to go with the sucky-sweets. But as we approached the tunnel, Ginger began telling me about how his neighbour had been thrown out of an upstairs window by his wife, who then reversed the car over him before emptying a tin of gloss paint over his clothes, which were in a pile on the front lawn, and setting light to them. The moral of the story was that I shouldn't be in such a panic because there's always someone worse off than myself. But the time flew by and before I knew it, we were out of le tunnel sous la Mange and had arrived in Calais.

Full of joie de vivre and several gin and tonics, a huge gust of wind caught Ginger as he stepped from the train and he lost his balance, unceremoniously landing in a clump on the platform. An old woman in her equal enthusiasm hadn't noticed and fell on top of him, bashing him on the head as she fell with her vanity case. After several minutes trying to untangle her gold bracelet from the back of his woolly hat, we realised that he had sprained his ankle. No dancing today for Fred and Ginger, then!

I helped him limp to a café near the concourse and we sat to drown our sorrows with a little breakfast.

'You would have been alright if you'd broken your ankle,' I mused to his disdain. 'Plaster of Paris must be cheaper in France?'

Ginger wasn't as impressed as our waitress Marie when I ordered my food in French, though I understood him being a little grumpy. So I didn't bother exasperating things further by admitting that I'd just ordered the only thing I know how to say in

French. As it turned out, Marie's real name was Mary and she was from Bolton, so I needn't have bothered.

After a couple of coffees, I hauled him back on the return train and we came home. Ironically, Claude the taxi driver from St Pancras was French, which just pissed Ginger off even more. Though to be fair, I have to admit, I was a little perturbed myself when I didn't get back what I'd paid for the Euros, thanks to a fluctuating exchange rate.

It transpired that Ginger had just sprained his ankle rather than broken it, which was a bonus. But some weeks later, he began trying to persuade me to revive our original plan and go back to France, by which time I'd gone off the idea. If I want to pay that much for a breakfast in the future, I think I'll go to Tiffany's!

MR CARTER'S LIBERATION

The first problem I had was my shoes. The precinct concourse was particularly slippery in the new stilettos I had bought to match the canary-yellow, feathered costume du jour. Walking up and down handing out leaflets to promote the recently re-fitted pet shop was proving difficult, despite my attempt to dress like one of the parrots in the shiny new window display.

'Rub a bit of coke, that oughta do it,' advised Sharine from the Belts & Buckles shop next door. If I were back in Soho rather than Hull, that may have meant something completely different. Some cotton wool soaked in Pepsi smeared across my soles did the trick, and flyers for "Heavy Petting" were literally flying out of my hands like there was no tomorrow. People were stopping to ask questions about the shop, and me, and we even had a little photo-call for the local rag. Sharine was delighted at their suggestion they mention it was next to Belts & Buckles and, being something of a local celebrity herself, jumped into one of the shots just in case. Though she did get quite ruffled when one of the baying onlookers called her Sharon.

Through all this fuss and nonsense, I noticed a tall middle-aged man in sensible grey clothing staring at me through horn-rimmed glasses from under a flat cap. Well, to be more accurate, it was my legs and tits he was looking at – nothing unusual for me at public appearances. I nodded at him, which is usually enough to deter unwanted gazes, but instead of him turning away as expected, his eyes twinkled and his smile widened.

Local press drama over, I was a little disconcerted to see him hanging around as the crowd slowly dispersed. After about five minutes, he seized his moment and approached.

'Some of us can just dream about it, but you… you're actually out there and doing it, aren't you?' he grinned. I was a bit confused.

'What, handing out leaflets?' I asked.

'No, cross-dressing! You're dressing as your true self in public… you know, out there in the field,' he nodded with glowing approval. 'Representing the hidden few. Widening the horizons of possibility. I'm very impressed.' Still confused, I offered him a leaflet. But he was otherwise distracted. He continued, 'All these years I've kept my secret. Oh, I've seen them on telly, but you're the first one I've actually met face-to-face.'

I looked to Sharon… sorry, Sharine for support, but she was close to bursting with laughter. Throwing a hand across her mouth to save embarrassment, she turned and ran back into Belts & Buckles, pulling at the back of her knickers as she fled. It was probably a good job she did. Putting down his Happy Shopper bags, the man leaned forward and rolled up his left trouser leg to above the knee. Standing back up, he gestured for me to look. Underneath his grey slacks and black socks, he was wearing ladies tan tights. Thick matted hair from his legs poked here and there through the tight nylon weave.

'Oh!' I gasped, a little taken aback by this sudden revelation. 'I see what you mean. Well, I actually only dress like this for work, but I know many people who do like to mix genders when they dress. I think you're very brave to show me, thank you very much!' I patted his arm sympathetically.

'Don't you just love the feel of a woman's bra stretched across your chest?' he sighed.

'Well, mostly I'm just glad to take it off when I've finished work, but that's not to say you shouldn't enjoy it.' There was a poignant silence before my curiosity finally got the better of me. 'Erm… are you wearing one now?' I asked delicately.

'Oh yes,' he answered proudly. 'Under my vest.' At that moment, a stern looking old lady in a sensible taupe raincoat and matching hat stopped beside us.

'For God's sake cover yourself up Mr Carter, making a show of yourself.' she cursed. 'Whatever you've got, we don't all want to see it.' Mr Carter looked a little embarrassed, though still defiant.

'What I've got, Mrs Finnigan, is pride. This young man has helped liberate me.' Mrs Finnigan looked me up and down with utter shock. I think, until that moment, she had been so distracted by Mr Carter's leg that she hadn't noticed I was a drag queen.

Face flushing a strange raspberry colour, she turned back to him, shouting, 'Our Valerie's been a vegetarian since August, but she doesn't go ramming it down everyone's throats in the precinct!' She turned on her heels and stomped off up the concourse, her mumblings of disapproval fading into the distance.

For a moment, Mr Carter looked broken. Then suddenly remembering himself, he hurriedly rolled his trouser leg back down. Before he could leave, I grabbed his wrist to get his attention.

'You know, you're not alone. There are many, many more who dress like you. Be happy, Mr Carter.' He smiled and patted my hand before picking up his shopping and scurrying away.

As I continued handing out leaflets, I pondered how difficult Mr Carter's secret life must be. Would there ever be a time when people like him wouldn't need to hide their true selves in public? Sadly, probably not in our lifetime.

IT'S ALL ABOUT CHROMALOIDS

There was a boy at my school who ate cat food. I guess at the time it made him feel a bit more important than he really was. Simon was his name and, like me, he was an outsider. We used to spend much of our time together during breaks sitting on the school field, where he would enthral me with his blueprint of how he would take over the world. Perhaps a useful person to know early on, if he'd succeeded. But then I was a little gullible and subsequently always drawn to eccentric people, cat breath or otherwise.

Some considerable years later, I was in a dressing room in Essex preparing for a drag performance. I was completing my makeover with a layer of lip-gloss when there was a knock at the door. Not yet in costume and half naked, I put on a dressing gown and answered. A small, stout balding man with greying hair to the sides and a long ginger beard stood outside, grinning broadly.

'Hello, Jeff! It's been such a long time,' he said, grasping my hand and shaking it enthusiastically.

'Hello,' I replied, a little unsure. 'I'm so sorry, you'll have to remind me... I'm not too good with names, faces, times and places. I wouldn't know my own knickers if they didn't have my name on!' He laughed, a little too heartily for the poor quality of the joke.

'It's me… Simon! You remember? We used to be in the same class at school?' In a flash I was fourteen again, sitting next to him in Biology. I could remember the orange Formica desks, the tatty, dusty skeleton on the hook in the corner and the strange smell emanating from the training farm that surrounded the Biology hut. The grief of using an umbrella to get to class when it was raining, and that little fat girl who had to be carried from the enclosure gate into lessons because the farm goose had taken a particular dislike to her. It was a certain squint in Simon's eye and his fidgety demeanour I remembered most, though I didn't recall him ever being ginger. He was like a miniature bobbing-head effigy of David Bellamy off someone's car dashboard. A brief chill ran down my spine when it dawned that this scruffy, little old man was the same age as me! I must confess I did take a bit of a sniff as he passed me to enter the room, but there was no longer a feline smell. Rather, a kind of musty odour, a bit like fresh putty.

'I've been watching you on telly,' he gushed. 'Who'd have thought, all them years ago when we used to sit on that wall outside the science huts?' I reminded him about his love of Whiskas and he reminded me that I used to eat rose petals from a recycled tobacco tin. I guess at the time it made me feel a bit more important, too. 'So, what are you doing now?' he smiled, before realising it was a bit of a daft question.

'What about you?' I asked in return.

'I'm the caretaker here at the Community Hall. I do all the maintenance and stuff.' Perhaps that's why he now smelt of putty. 'Do you ever keep in touch with any of the old gang?' he asked. I was never aware that there had been an old gang. Perhaps he'd had an old gang that I knew nothing about? 'Do you remember old Susan, who nearly drowned during swimming lessons?' I shook my head. 'Or Kevin, who got that big gash up his leg on the back football field?' His extraordinary memory recall seemed a bit gory to me.

'No, sorry. I haven't kept in touch with anyone from those days. Anyway, I doubt they'd remember me now.'

'Well, I did!' he answered, almost a little offended. Uncomfortable, I decided to change the subject.

'Are you married, Simon?'

'Not anymore.' Oh. That didn't work!

'Erm... so what do you do with yourself, nowadays?'

'I've been investigating Chromaloids,' he said, rubbing his chin intelligently.

'Chromaloids?' I didn't remember learning anything about them in Biology.

'Yes. I've got a rabbit with five legs. I think it's something to do with its geneticism. Some kind of latent mutation, as though a new breed is being secretly developed. It's MI5. They don't want us to know what's really going on. It's a conspiracy, and it's all about Chromaloids. Have you heard of the Illuminati?'

It would normally have been about now that I'd have called for security. But realising that as caretaker, he probably was the security, I had to think of a different tact. 'Erm... this is a lovely venue, you're obviously very good at your job.'

'It keeps me out of any more trouble,' he twitched, poking a finger into the side of his grubby trainer to scratch.

'Well, I must be getting into costume now, Simon,' I suggested, as he sniffed at his retrieved digit. 'Nice to meet you again!' I fibbed, encouraging him to the door.

As I drove home after the performance, I thought about the kind of life that poor rabbit must have with Simon. And I thought about my school; the seventies bell-bottomed trousers and black nylon blazer. Endless stone-floored corridors and the smell of fresh paint at the start of a new term. And pure elation at walking out through its cold, concrete doorway for the last time and into the bright, exciting possibilities of my future life. I'm grateful for the basic knowledge it gave me, but I'm glad that no links with its former inhabitants remain.

IN DOUGHNUTS AND WAR

I'm not one for eating while walking, as a rule. Aside from the practical choreography of getting everything where it should be - in your mouth and not down the front of your coat - it had been drummed into me on more than one occasion that it can be seen as rather common. But of course, when facing the temptation of getting all the way home from the shops without sinking into a fresh, soft jam doughnut, there are different priorities.

Licking sugar from my lips, I walked from the escalators out onto the roof of the precinct and across the car park, looping my shopping bag handle onto my elbow so I could pull the car keys from my pocket. Pressing my key fob, the bleep from my car's central locking attracted the attention of a swooping seagull. It lunged in the direction of my doughnut with such force that it blew the end of my scarf back over my shoulder. I was horrified at how enormous it was and a little surprised that it was there at all, being some twenty miles from the coast. My instant reaction was to run, but in the drama of it all, I dropped my keys. Crouching to retrieve them, a sinister chill ran down my spine. Lifting my face to glance ahead, I realised the creature had landed and we were now eye to eye. This was war.

Instinctively, I threw the last mouthful of my doughnut as far across the car park as I possibly could. As it left my hand, the seagull snapped at it as if to catch. The loud crack of its enormous empty beak had the sound of bone breaking.

'That could have been my arm!' I gasped, as I leapt to my feet and ran for the car. But my nemesis had collected his payoff and returned in no time at all. I could hear the sound of his wings flapping as I lunged into the driver seat and slammed the door shut.

For a fleeting moment, it appeared that he had given up and moved on to his next hapless victim. But then I could hear him walking about on my roof. I lay silently draped across the passenger seat, listening with the fear of someone discovering an intruder in their house.

'Just drive away!' I told myself, but the seagull had other ideas. As I sat up in my seat, he jumped down onto my bonnet and stared diligently into my eyes from the other side of the windscreen. He knew there were more doughnuts in my bag, and he wasn't going to give up now. With a loud squawk, he tapped aggressively on my windscreen. I turned on my engine and tooted my horn several times to scare him. Feathers unruffled, he retaliated by pulling up one of my windscreen wipers and nudging it with the side of his head, as if to break it off. He wanted me out of the car… he wanted my remaining doughnuts!

I jolted the car forward a couple of feet to shake him off. Lunging towards me, he banged his head on the windshield before sliding backwards across the bonnet and dropping onto the road in front of me. I was now trapped on all sides in my parking space. His enormous head popped back into view over the front of my bonnet. I was about to learn that Hell has no fury like a seagull scorned. He screeched loudly, relentlessly, again and again, over and over without breaking his gaze for a moment. This wasn't just anger, this was a battle cry!

Suddenly he stopped. Gradually through the deafening silence that followed, I could sense the sound of something approaching, like the evil winged monkeys from The Wizard of Oz. Two, then three, then four of his gang arrived, surrounding the car like black-winged vultures waiting to pick at my bones... and my remaining doughnuts. Tooting my horn had no effect; they'd fought this battle before. For six long minutes I sat there terrorised until some other unsuspecting shopper walked out with a bag of chips, distracting them away. Seizing my moment, I threw the car into gear and tore away.

I did feel for the poor unsuspecting woman. By the time I'd reached the car park's exit ramp, I could see in my rearview mirror that her battle had already begun. But in doughnuts and war, sometimes it's every man for himself.

HAPPY CAMPING

When I sat on the long, brightly coloured bench against the side window, the room tipped to one side and my plastic cup slid off the table. As it crashed to the floor, coffee splashed everywhere and began a long trail down the tatty wood-effect Lino towards the bedroom. Grasping at the matching flowery curtains in shock, I shouted, 'What the bugger's going on?'

'Oh, I forgot to tell you. The ground dips under that back corner of the caravan,' said Fred, the campsite manager. I wasn't impressed.

'Well, what am I supposed to do?'

'Best stay up this end,' he advised, as though subsidence is something I should have already anticipated. Grabbing the end of the Formica table, which was thankfully bolted to the floor, I pulled myself back into a standing position. The room lunged back to where it had begun. Fred pulled an oily looking rag from his back pocket and wiped his forehead. Then stooping, he began mopping up the coffee. 'Anyways, the disco's in that hut over the back there.' He pointed in a vague direction through one wall. 'Wayne... that's the DJ, starts at seven-thirty, so if you want to start your turn at about nine, that would be smashing!' He stood and blew his nose on the now sodden cloth before plunging it back into his pocket.

'Are you sure there's nowhere in the hut I can get ready?' I asked.

'Well, you're better off here in this van,' he smiled. 'It's better equipped and a bit more watertight.' Looking around at the nineteen-sixty's interior, I dreaded to think what kind of a mess the hut must be in. I grabbed my suitcase and headed towards the bedroom.

'It won't tip up again if I go in here, will it?' I asked, cautiously.

'No you'll be fine, just stay away from that far corner.

The bedroom was darker with the curtains drawn. Pulling them back to let in a little of the early evening light, I turned to find a chicken lounging on the bed. 'There's something in here you might like to take with you, Fred,' I called.

'Ah, there you are, Drumstick,' he said, almost affectionately. Scooping her up into his arms, he left me to unpack. I shook the stray feathers off of the quilt and laid out my suitcase. Thankfully it was just a dressing room; I wasn't staying the night.

A couple of hours later, I was made up and in costume, ready to begin the show. I could hear a loud rumbling noise, like a train approaching. It took me a while to figure out that it was the sound of rain hammering on the roof of the caravan. Fabulous! A full-length pink sequinned gown and hand-curled blonde wig... and a hurricane-flooded quagmire to cross to reach the hut. Fred duly arrived with an umbrella and a pair of green wellington boots for me to slip into. Frock draped over my arm and sling-backs in hand, I clasped the back of Fred's jacket and squelched in his wake across to the brightly illuminated clubhouse.

Arriving in the entrance lobby, I ducked briefly into the gent's toilet to put my shoes back on and re-adjust myself in several places, which was a bit of a shock for one elderly man as he exited the cubical. One look at me with my hand up my skirt and his jaw hit the floor before he turned back into the cubicle and locked himself in.

Everything back where it was intended, Fred led me down a dark corridor to one side of the hall. It had been created by a curtain dividing us from the waiting audience - the idea being that my stepping straight out onto the stage would have a bigger impact than being seen loitering in the corner waiting for my entrance music. There was a distinct smell of damp dog, which I soon realised was Fred's jacket. I sniffed the hand that had earlier been grasping the back of it. I needed to remember to do the joke where I put my finger in my mouth with my other hand.

Reaching the side of the stage and looking across, I could see Wayne standing behind his DJ stand at the opposite end. He looked as though he was about to cry. I was beginning to understand why. Looking up, he spotted me and waved my show cd in the air above his head, as if to advise that he was ready for my signal to begin. Squinting through the dry-smoke billowing across the floor, I thought I could see his teeth. Perhaps really he was smiling but just had one of those depressive faces.

As my opening music leapt from the speakers, I put one foot onto the stage ready to step up. 'Oh, by the way,' whispered Fred, 'the woodblock's just been polished.' Too late. My foot slid half a metre onto the stage, and the opening lines of my first song began with me practically doing the splits. The audience of course thought it was all very funny, so I picked myself up and carried on. My first big spin was a bit tricky. On my way round, I noticed a black plastic bucket half-full of dripping rainwater to one side of Wayne's equipment. My second spin wasn't quite as successful. Sliding rapidly backwards through the smoke, I kicked the bucket and splashed water across a row of multi-plug extension leads on the floor in front of the disco lights. With a flash and a loud bang, my music abruptly stopped and the entire hall was plunged into darkness. Everybody cheered.

I had to wait twenty minutes for them to mop up by torchlight and switch the electricity back on. A request to return and perform again the following month before the end of the rainy season was politely declined.

ENTER AT YOUR OWN PERIL

Technology is a wonderful thing. It has changed almost every aspect of our lives in so many ways, making us wonder how we ever survived without it. Of course we did survive, though things were often a little more complicated. On the day I moved into my new house in London, I was still waiting for my telephone service to be switched on. Mobile phones had been invented but were the size of house bricks and still rare playthings of wealthy City bankers. Not fortunate enough to have one of my own, I had to find a call box to discover why my van of furniture hadn't yet arrived.

Luckily, through the cold February downpour, I discovered one at the end of the street. It was a big old red cast iron number, originally issued by the Post Office. Armed with a handful of loose change, I pulled at the door. It took two or three tugs to get the bloody thing open. Clearly it had been overlooked on several maintenance runs.

Jumping inside out of the rain, the first thing that hit me was a hideously pungent smell. It was sadly a kiosk that doubled as a public toilet. I wondered how Superman would have coped had he leapt in for a quick change. Perhaps the water running off my clothes would give it a quick rinse through, I thought. With one eye on the road in case my elusive van drove by, I grappled for the removal company's card and picked up the receiver. The line was dead. It was then that I noticed a bunch of fine, multi-coloured wires yanked from underneath the box. The vandal had clearly needed something to occupy his mind while he was emptying his bladder! I pushed at the door to exit, now desperate for a gasp of fresh air. It was jammed solid. I frantically tried the other walls to be sure that I was pushing at the right one, but still nothing. Putting the change back into my pocket, I put my back to it and pushed my feet against the opposite wall in an attempt to add some force, but it refused to budge.

It was at this moment I noticed a little grey and white cat, sheltering from the rain under an overhang of ivy to the ragged brick wall behind. He watched with silent contempt as I struggled for oxygen in my urine-soaked prison.

'Go and get help!' I cried through a small hole in one of the glass panels. He ignored my pleas, deciding instead to sit and take in the unfolding drama. My attention turned to passersby in the street. The heavy rain seemed to be drowning the sound of my shouting, making it hard to get a response from any of the scurrying pedestrians, with their coat collars up and heads down. Finally, I got the attention of an elderly lady in a lilac coat and plastic rain hat.

'Eh?' she shouted, parking her shopping trolley to one side.

'I can't get out, can you please get some help?' I pleaded.

'No, dear,' she replied with a squint, 'it doesn't work.' At that moment, my van cruised slowly past, looking for me to flag them down from my new front gate.

'Stop that van!' I gasped, pointing. By the time she'd turned to look, the van had gone. But, following the direction of my pointing, she grabbed her trolley and wandered off across the road and up the turning opposite, as if she'd somehow find the answer to what I was so desperate to convey.

A pit of despair developed in my stomach. It was nearly five-thirty and I knew my furniture drop was the last one of the day. What if they couldn't find me, gave up and went home? I'd spend the night sleeping on bare floorboards... or worse, suffocating in the telephone urinal. Panic set in.

'Help! Help!' I screamed, banging as loudly as I could on the windows. My van went round again. I was desperate! At that moment, a middle-aged man in a green trench coat ducked under the ivy to light a cigarette. I banged loudly on the glass to his side, screaming through the hole. He jumped a foot into the air, not expecting to be confronted with my verbal onslaught. Taking a long drag on his rollup to ensure it was properly lit, he walked around to the door handle and casually pulled it open. I lunged out, gasping for air.

'Yeah it gets stuck from the inside, mate. Happens all the time. Nearly every night they find a drunk standing in his own puddle.' He glanced me up and down briefly, perhaps trying to assess if I was one of those unfortunate folk.

'I was just trying to use the phone,' I explained, not wishing my potential new neighbour to think of me in such a lowly way.

'It don't work,' he offered, usefully. Suddenly, my van went round for a third time.

'Thanks so much,' I said before running up the street after my furniture.

Once all my belongings had dried of rainwater, I could finally settle into my new home. My phone was now working, washing machine plumbed in and everything relatively hunky dory. There was just one more job to do. I walked back down to my former cell of incarceration at the end of the street. The little grey and white cat was in his usual place. Seeing me coming, he scarpered over the wall, perhaps anticipating revenge for his complacency. I shuddered, briefly recalling my hour of terror before posting a large white sign on the side of the phone box, which read, "Enter At Your Own Peril".

EIGHT MINUTES

I stood at the bus stop in Lewisham High Street trying to decide whether or not to just go home. I hadn't come by bus as I only lived walking distance away, but had arranged to meet Cynthia nearly an hour beforehand. Finally, a bus pulled in and out she stepped.

'It's fashionable for a bride to be late,' she exclaimed without the expected apology.

'But you're not a bride,' I replied, 'you haven't even snared a fiancé yet. I really don't know why you're looking for a wedding dress.' She stared at me tetchily for a moment, trying to read from my expression if I would still shop with her. As a drag queen, she seemed to think I would be some kind of expert.

'I need to plan ahead,' she snapped. 'At my age, when I find a man, I've got to get on with it bloody quickly, before he changes his mind and buggers off again.' If this ever-elusive groom did bugger off, it would be because of her attitude and not her age, I thought. But sensing her stress, I grabbed her arm and began walking her towards the precinct.

'Come on then, let's get this over with.'

As we entered Mrs Bliss's Wedding Emporium, Cynthia's face lit up like a dog in a biscuit shop. Row upon row of every kind of dress in every shade of white, cream and beige lined the walls. She ran her hand across the front of them excitedly, as though she had a ceremony planned for each one. A snooty yet immaculately groomed middle-aged shop assistant appeared, glancing down her long bony nose at Cynthia's hands to ensure they were clean.

'Can I help you, Modom,' she snarled disapprovingly, assessing Cynthia's appearance before gesturing towards the budget section to one side.

'I'm getting married and need something very special for my Mr Perfect.' Cynthia gushed. 'He's a captain in the Air Force and we're expecting titled people at the church.'

'Really?' asked the assistant disbelievingly, glancing at me for confirmation. I just shrugged. It was already all I could do to keep a straight face. Looking discreetly at her watch, Mrs Bliss pulled out a huge puffy number and hung it across the front of the rail for approval. I had to chuckle that the first dress was dark cream and not white; she had clearly read Cynthia like a book before she'd even tried anything on.

'If Modom would like to experience this creation in the fitting room, we might establish Modom's further requirements,' she suggested. Cynthia's excitement turned to embarrassment when she saw the label.

'This is a size eighteen, I'm only a fourteen!'

'Of course you are Modom, but we are merely establishing a style that Modom would suit,' she advised, hastily guiding Cynthia and her dress into a curtained off area to one corner. Bride out of sight, I couldn't help but laugh. But as Mrs Bliss stepped from the changing area, she caught me. I expected her to be angry, but instead she smiled the smile of an ally.

'I've worked here for thirty years,' she whispered, dropping her upper-crust accent a little. Then looking at her watch again, she gestured, 'eight minutes.' I smiled approvingly, fascinated by the suggested challenge. I admired her choreographed elegance as she glided across the thick pile carpet to the reception desk and scribbled something on a piece of paper. Suddenly, Cynthia appeared from behind the curtain. The dress fitted her perfectly, considering it was allegedly several sizes too big. Mrs Bliss gasped, throwing her hand to her chest and grasping the side of the counter to steady her balance.

'Oh Modom,' she exclaimed, taking a small piece of tissue from her sleeve and holding it to her nose. 'It's a dream!' Cynthia was delighted, running across the room to a large gold-framed mirror. Instantly regaining her composure, Mrs Bliss hurried behind to fluff the back of the frock. I smiled and shook my head with respect for her impeccably scripted routine. She was top of the bill, upstaging the bride completely, and the shop floor was her stage.

'Do you really think so?' gushed Cynthia.

'Thousands of blushing brides have crossed my threshold and yet I don't think I've ever seen such a perfect match. Would Modom mind if I took a photograph for our catalogue?' Cynthia was thrilled, striking a pose as the assistant took a few imaginary snaps from a camera that clearly had no film in it. 'I've written the name of the dress on a piece of paper for Modom. There is no model number because it's a one off, the only one made before the seamstress eloped to Romania with her gypsy lover.'

'Oh my,' sighed Cynthia romantically, 'what's it called?'

'Fairy Tale Princess,' announced Mrs Bliss, with a well-trodden tearful wobble in her voice. Cynthia burst into tears, pulling her into a hug. She checked her watch again behind Cynthia's back. I nodded my approval, though I was merely in a supporting role.

As we stepped from the shop, I turned to glance back at Mrs Bliss, turning the door sign to "closed" and pulling down the blind. Catching my glance, she paused momentarily and gently smiled at me with a wink. I checked my watch: eight minutes exactly.

I've always aspired to be as good on stage as those who shine with genius. That cloudy afternoon in Lewisham, we had been in the presence of a master.

DEPTFORD WIVES

The A40 in London was jammed solid, as usual. It was a long way to travel from home and took a big chunk of my day but, before the wonders of the internet, the best place to buy wigs for my cabaret show had always been directly from the wholesalers. I ran through in my mind what I needed as I finally pulled into the car park. A replacement Cher, a spare Kate Bush and something suitable for a new impersonation, Sophie Ellis-Bextor, as well as anything else I fancied the look of.

As I stepped from my car, an open-topped blue Mercedes parked nose-to-nose with me. Out stepped two over-groomed middle-aged women. They appeared to have just arrived from the fictional town of Stepford. That is, until one of them spoke.

'My drawers have gone right up my crack,' moaned the redhead with a grapple around her lower regions. Hmm, more Deptford than Stepford, I thought. Gathering up my reference photos from the passenger seat, I followed them inside.

By the time I'd pushed through the swing doors to the industrial shelved display area, they had already taken the place over. Through a gap between two wig-adorned mannequin heads, I peered at them in the next aisle where, in louder than necessary voices, they read a list from a diamante Filo-fax.

'And we need a couple of striking numbers you can gander from a distance, for the window,' said the blonde. I assumed they had some kind of shop.

As I turned a corner, I spied a display head with a very short ginger wig. I stood looking at it for a moment, pondering whether it would be good for an early Annie Lennox caricature. Suddenly, the redhead stepped blatantly in front of me, took Annie's head from the shelf and walked off with it, shouting, 'What about this one, Lynne?' She clearly considered her own need far greater than mine. I coughed – as much from her overpowering perfume as to draw attention to her bad manners. 'What?' she snapped back at me. I nodded to a large green sign that requested mannequins remain on the shelf and to ask for assistance if you want a closer look. 'I've got a business to run,' she scolded.

'So have I,' I replied. Her heel squeaked on the Lino as she spun to face me.

'Listen, mate. Our Edgware emporium, with solarium, sauna and an extensive array of treatments and product for hair and beauty, supports people whose hair's fell out after chemo. We provide an important service to the community. Do you want to deny a sick person of that?' It sounded scripted and rehearsed to me. Clearly, I wasn't the first person to have ever questioned their behavior.

'And you're providing someone on chemotherapy with a cropped ginger comedy wig?' I asked. At this moment, a sales assistant arrived.

'Is there a problem?' he asked nervously.

'No problem,' I replied, 'But I'd like to buy that wig.' I pointed to Annie, still clasped in the woman's hand. He too pointed to the green sign. With a loud tut, she returned it to its rightful position on the shelf.

'What do you want it for, anyway?' she said, looking me up and down as though I'd just stepped off a farmyard tractor.

'Annie Lennox,' I said. 'I'm a female impersonator.' She looked me up and down again, then back up at the wig. Instantly, her demeanour changed.

'You have it then, with my blessing,' she smiled. I had already decided that was a foregone conclusion. 'And here's our card,' she said, producing something gold and glittery from the back of her Filofax. I carefully plucked it from amongst her extraordinarily manicured talons. 'We cater for drag queen wigs, too.' Not wishing to prolong our pained exchange by pointing out the obvious, I quickly fulfilled my own wholesale list, put some silver in a Marie Curie pot on the sales counter, and left them to it.

BRIDGET'S CASTLE

"DRAG QUEEN" screamed the sign, written in blood-red lipstick across three wrinkled sheets of kitchen roll. I assumed this was probably for my benefit. I saw it as soon as I stepped from the train, as did most of the other passengers. By the time I had shown my ticket and manoeuvred my bags and cases through the narrow check point, a small crowd had gathered to see who would turn up. Perhaps they were expecting me to come somersaulting through dressed as Carmen Miranda. They looked almost disappointed as I approached my collection point.

'Hello, I'm Jeff,' I smiled.

'Who?' said the fat, middle-aged man with a broad Lancashire accent. He pushed back his flat cap, blinking heavily through his re-entry shield horn-rimmed glasses.

'The Drag Queen?'

'Oh. You'd best come with, then,' he frowned, looking a little dejected himself. He turned to his crowd and shrugged, screwing the tissue into a ball. Fifteen minutes of notoriety over, he took one of my cases and turned, beckoning me to follow him towards a bright shaft of daylight reflecting across the concourse. 'Welcome to Blackpool,' he frowned, wiping his nose on the ball of kitchen roll before shoving it into his beige coat pocket. 'I had your proper name written on a sheet of paper, but a gust of wind took it out the car window on the roundabout, so

I had to improvise.' I didn't like to ask if the red lipstick was his. 'The name's Bernard. It's the wife's guest house really, I just do as I'm told,' he winced, glancing at me in the rear-view mirror of his equally beige Hillman Minx. 'Bridget; the love of my life... so she tells me,' he said with an ironic, suppressed tone. I was already looking forward to meeting her!

'It's very kind of you to collect me from the station, Bernard. I'm very grateful,' I said, peering out from amongst my bags on the back seat.

'I've had my orders. There's no room for bags in the boot; I had to do Budgens on the way. That's tomorrow's breakfast back there with the spare tyre.'

Attempting to climb out from my luggage onto such a steeply-sloped pavement was a challenge I hadn't prepared myself for.

'For Christ's sake Bernard, don't just stand there like a wet weekend in Cleveleys, help the poor man! You can see he's struggling,' came a steely, northern female voice from somewhere above my head. As Bernard lifted the biggest suitcase from my lap, I looked up... and there she was! At the head of a run of concrete steps, leaning against the porch of an enormous, multi-story Victorian bed and breakfast, stood Bridget. Playtex tits pointed defiantly through a tight coral-pink jersey, draped from the matching flared nylon slacks by a gold loop belt. A huge platinum-blonde hairpiece clung atop a violently pulled-back fringe, framed by dangly gold ball earrings big enough to play tennis with. She batted her massive eyelashes and flicked her cigarette holder, kicking aside the fallen ash with a well-trodden gold platform shoe. Then, blowing her fag smoke upwards into the seaside-flavoured Blackpool air, she spoke.

'Hello, chuck. Welcome to Bridget's Castle!' She threw her arms into the air with a broad, yellow grin. She was more of a drag queen than I could ever aspire to be! Then back to the car, she threw an acid glance and growled, 'Bernard! Get them bags up to that third floor and take your coat off, them potatoes won't peel themselves.' With a glance up and down the street to ensure we'd had an audience, she spun on her heels and disappeared inside.

Bridget's Castle was a time capsule of nineteen seventies kitsch. Large patterned multi-coloured wallpapers clashed aggressively with equally overwhelming carpets. A smell of stale cigarette smoke and long since eaten fried bacon hung nostalgically in the air.

'This is the lounge,' she gestured proudly, as we entered a massive, high ceilinged room overlooking the front elevation. Four tired flowery sofas stood amongst an immense collection of ornamental ceramic poodles.

'I like me dogs, as you can see,' she said, lifting a particularly pink one and flicking the dust from the shelf beneath. 'They're my babies, really. I've got two – Dilly and Dally, you'll meet them later.' I could already smell them. 'Now, I know you've got the show at the Labour Club every night this week and you'll probably be finishing late, so come and go as you please, I'll give you a key.'

'Thank you, that's thoughtful,' I said.

'Smoke if you like but use an ashtray. And I'm OK with dalliances and gentlemen callers. I'm very open-minded like that, me. I'm a big fan of Dale Winton and I had that George Michael sussed before anybody else up the street.' She took a long draw on her cigarette, glowing in her remembered glory. 'Think of this as a home from home, a taste of the real Blackpool. You're in number thirteen on the third floor. I'll bring you up a cup of tea in a bit and have a look at your frocks.' She looked around to check we were alone and dropped to a whisper. 'Only, stick them in the wardrobe and keep the key in your handbag, or you'll have Bernard up there trying them on when you're out.' So that was Bernard's red lipstick, after all. It was going to be an eventful week!

ALVIN'S BALCONY

As I pulled into the car park, I could see him leaning precariously out of the fourth-floor window. He was waving something tied to the end of a long stick outside the window of next door's flat.

'Alvin?' I shouted. He jumped with shock, dropping the stick and grabbing the outside of his window frame to stop himself from plunging. There was a crashing sound as his apparatus disappeared from view behind the ground floor flat's garden fence.

There was no lift to Alvin's floor, so I was a little puffed by the time I reached his front door. He answered in dark glasses, grabbing me by the sleeve of my jacket and pulling me in, slamming the door shut behind me.

'What the hell's going on?' I asked, still worried from his frantic phone call to me earlier that afternoon.

'It's all getting out of hand! I'm not sure how much longer I can cope,' he grizzled. 'And to top it all, I think my mirror on a stick has just knocked the head off Mr Finch's garden gnome.'

'Sit down,' I comforted with a warm hug, 'and I'll put the kettle on. And take those silly glasses off!'

'There's been eight so far this week, and it's only Tuesday,' said Alvin, standing from his kitchen table for a third time to peer through his nets.

'Eight what? And what were you doing with that mirror on a stick?'

'Eight men. I was trying to see what they're doing. She's got one in there now!' I was shocked.

'Come and drink your tea,' I scolded. 'I've brought Battenberg especially, because you said you was stressed.' Disgruntled, he returned and slumped into his chair like a spoilt child.

'I know they're going to her because I can hear them. Besides which, there's only two flats past my window on this balcony, hers and old Mrs Cullfeathers' on the end, and nobody ever visits Mrs Cullfeathers. She's a nasty bit of work.' He blew across the top of his tea, dipping his little finger in to fish out a stray tealeaf before taking a sip.

'What do you mean, you can hear them?' I asked.

'Well, if I kneel on my bed with my ear above the headboard, there's talking. Though I'm not sure what they're saying, even with a glass against the wall.' I couldn't quite believe what I was hearing.

'You can't do that! It's a severe invasion of privacy. How would you like it if she did it to you?'

'I tell you,' he growled, slamming both hands on the table, 'there's something not right going on in there and I intend to get to the bottom of it. For all I know, it could be bringing down the tone of the whole block!' It sounded a bit hypocritical to me, but he was clearly very distraught.

'OK, I'll help you investigate, but only if it puts an end to this outrageous nosey parkering. You're too old for all this!'

After scouting all the local phone boxes to see if we could find a card with her picture on (his idea, not mine), we decided to have a vigil in the car park. It was the only way to be sure that this army of gentlemen callers were not all a just a figment of Alvin's imagination. I was mindful that he was, after all, a dear friend who had been there for me through more than one crisis of my own.

I had repositioned my car to face the stairs and Alvin's balcony. From our vantage point, we could see most of the car park, the entrance to the staircase and everybody's front doors. He had made a flask of hot cocoa and some cheese and cucumber sandwiches, and we still had a couple of slices of Battenberg left. Wrapped in coats with blankets across our legs to keep off the chill as dusk fell, we settled in for what could be a long wait.

'The Council didn't want to know,' he said, nervously fidgeting with his camera phone. 'And the letters I sent to the other flats in the block didn't come to anything, either. Except that dirty old pervert two floors below me, who wrote back asking if I had her phone number.' I looked at him, patiently. He sighed. 'You think I'm mad, don't you? Perhaps I am. I guess I've just been so vexed since I was burgled last year. It stresses me to know there's all and sundry passing my front door. And if I can hear her, she can probably hear me, or more to the point, knows when I'm not there. For all I know, it could have been her and one of her fancy bits who robbed me!'

I could see his concern. But the moment was fleeting. Suddenly, a dark figure did indeed leave through his neighbour's front door, heading towards the stairs.

'Quick,' cried Alvin, ready to leap from his seat, 'block his exit with the car, I'm gonna have him!' I grabbed him by the back of the jacket and pulled him back in.

'No, you're too emotional. Stay here, I'll go and talk to him.' The multitudes of men Alvin had imagined were actually just two, his neighbour's brothers. They had been visiting her daily because she too was stressed after hearing about Alvin's robbery.

Relieved of his cynicism, the following day he invited her in for a cup of tea and the remains of the Battenberg. Mr Finch found a new garden gnome on his doorstep. And having joined forces with the remaining tenants in the block, they now have a secure entry door at the bottom of their communal stairwell.

A DRAWER FULL OF CHEESE

'I'm so pleased you could make it! I'm always watching you on there,' sighed Melinda, referring to my recent bit of telly. She adjusted her silk head-scarf, looking down at her shiny plastic Wellington boots dejectedly. 'You're good company for me since Dexter moved in with that woman. She's from India. I'm practically running the business alone while he's round there licking the red dot off her forehead!' Oh dear.

Lifting my suitcase, I followed her across the station car park to her tired-looking green Land Rover. 'So, tell me about the business you want me to open for you,' I asked optimistically, as I fastened my seat belt.

'We've had the shop for about three years and we're doing very well there.' She threw the car violently into reverse and shot backwards, adding, 'Well, I'm doing very well there. Frankly I don't see him that often since he started eating Indian take-away.' I bit into my tongue and looked out of the window, trying to prevent my creeping smile from further complicating an already fraught journey.

Following a ten-minute silence, her mood lightened as we turned towards the main high street.

'The reason I've asked you here today is for you to re-open for us as we've had a re-fit. The local rag will be there and a bunch of our regulars. I'd like you to cut the ribbon, as it were, and perhaps just say a few words?'

'Sounds like fun,' I replied, relieved the cloud of doom had lifted.

'You will be in costume, won't you? In your drag?'

'Yes, no problem. It's all in here,' I replied, tapping the side of my bag. 'What kind of shop do you have?' I asked.

Pulling into a designated space to the back of a row of shops, she snapped off her seat belt and turned to face me. With a big toothy grin, she gushed, 'Cheese!'

Following her back out of the parking area and around the end building to the high street, I was a little mystified. 'Can I just ask… why did you book a drag queen to re-launch a cheese shop?'

She laughed, a little too much for comfort. 'Well, it is rather cheesy isn't it really? Don't you think? A man, singing in a bra and high heels?' I could see her train of logic, unhinged as it may be. 'Here we are,' she smiled proudly, turning the key to a small vintage glass-paned door.

I have to say, the shop interior was lovely. White marble-topped counters adorned with protective glass shields separated us from beautiful buttermilk-painted Edwardian shelves with panelling below. A huge brass and crystal lantern hung high up in the centre of the room, casting a gentle glow over the terracotta tiled floor. And a rainbow of different coloured cheese as far as the eye could see.

'I'm going to put you in the back room,' she said, directing me through a small door to one corner. 'It's our office, really. There's a big mirror, as you requested, and the toilet has a sink. There's no shower, I'm afraid. Is that OK?' As I entered, it hit me like a house brick in the face. Perhaps the most nauseating smell I had ever encountered. Melinda noticed my face screwing. 'It's the smell, isn't it?' she guessed, apologetically. I couldn't speak for a moment as it hit the back of my throat. I hadn't noticed any smell at all back in the shop. She opened a window and poured me a glass of water as I coughed. 'It's him,' she scowled. 'Look!' She pulled open a wooden dresser drawer to reveal a small collection of blue mouldy lumps.

'Ergh, what is it?' I grimaced.

'I told him. People in the high street aren't interested in exotic blends anymore. But oh no, he knows best, doesn't he? We must keep them just in case, mustn't we? I'm a fool to myself listening to him.' I'm not sure I'd ever seen anyone so emotional about cheese.

'Oh,' I whispered, not sure how to respond.

'He may have taken a fancy to the exotic, but it's not for me. It's no good, I can't take it anymore!' Plunging her hands into the drawer, she grasped several furry lumps and launched them out of the open window. Realising that much of the goo was still clinging to the bottom of the drawer, she ripped it from its runners and threw that out, too. I sensed from her air of long-awaited achievement that its disposal had an underlying meaning, as though a weight had lifted from her shoulders. 'Right,' she said with a smile, squirting a glob of liquid soap into her hands and running them under the tap. 'I'll pop the kettle on, we've got about an hour.'

The ribbon cut itself was quite fun. By chance, I'd brought a yellow frock which, with the blond wig, gave me the look of a deranged Dairy Queen. I cut the ribbon to a ripple of polite applause from local shoppers and posed for a few photos.
'Cheese!' My client Melinda was happy and everything was going swimmingly... until Dexter arrived. On his arm was a well-dressed attractive young woman with beautiful long black hair. She looked more like a well-tanned government minister than the subservient native sari-adorned immigrant from Melinda's description. Her thunder stolen, Melinda blended into the crowd as Dexter passed glasses of wine to the Press.

Back on the train and relieved to be on my way home, I looked down at the brown paper and string-wrapped thank you gift Melinda had given me. With little hesitation, I lobbed it out of the train window. I'd had enough cheese for one day.

TWO SAUSAGES

'I can't wait, I'm on a double yellow line. Here, cop hold of this for a minute.' I span in my dressing-room chair to glance over my shoulder. Although that evening's show was finished, I was still in full costume, makeup and wig. I wasn't expecting anyone to burst in through the door, at least without first knocking.

I had recognised the voice as that of Charmaine, or "Cranky Char" as our mutual friends had secretly named her. We had only recently been introduced and I hadn't known her long, so was surprised when she offered to collect me after my show and take me home. She'd explained it would save me money on my taxi, the journey would be a chance for us to get to know each other better and she would be able to see where I lived. But as I turned, Charmaine was nowhere to be seen. Instead, I was confronted by a small person. A little girl with a lollipop and a dog, to be precise.

'Hello! What's your name?' I asked gently.

'My daddy says that you're really a man and that you're only pretending to be a woman,' she blurted, nervously. I couldn't help but laugh, which made the dog growl at me.

'Well yes, but I only pretend when I'm at work. I don't do it all the time.' She screwed her eyes into a squint as she pondered her next move, while taking another big slurp of her lollipop.

'Are you working now?' she asked.

'No, I've just finished.'

'Then why haven't you changed into a man again?' She edged backwards slowly towards the corner of the room, dragging the hapless little mongrel with her. As she stopped by the window, her raised lollipop stuck to the curtain. Perhaps realising it would now be covered in fluff, she let go of it and left it there, hanging.

'I'll get changed in a minute or two. How old are you?' I asked.

'I'm six and three-twelfths and my name's Tilly, to answer your other question.'

'Ah, right,' I smiled. 'Why don't you come and sit down while we're waiting?' As I stood to lift a chair from the stack stored against the back wall, the dog began barking at me incessantly.

'Stop it, Terminator!' she scolded, pulling him back by the lead.

'Terminator? That's a fierce name for such a little dog!' I laughed.

'Yes well, that's because he's a very fierce dog, considering he's only four,' she replied proudly.

The door suddenly flew open again. This time it was Dom, the venue's manager. 'What on earth's going on?' he shouted.

'Don't anyone knock in this place?' I whinged over the noise.

'You ain't got nothing I ain't seen before, you old crab,' he bitched. 'What's that?' he said, pointing disapprovingly at Tilly and her deranged companion.

'This is my friend's daughter and that's her pet.

'There's no kids allowed in my bar. Or dogs!' He stamped his foot. 'And what's that?' He pointed at the lollipop hanging on the curtain. Terminator was relentless.

'Kill!' I instructed, as it lunged towards him. With a hysterical cry, he ran back out, slamming the door behind him.

'I told you he was fierce, didn't I?' said Tilly, with a toothless grin. 'But if I can just give you a word of advice if this ever happens again?' She spoke with distinct authority for such a small person. 'Try this!' She reached into her pocket and pulled out two sausages. Terminator instantly stopped yapping and sat timidly at her feet, staring up expectantly and licking his lips. 'Now,' she said. 'I'm going to give him just half a sausage now and save the other half for just in case something else will happen.'

'Good idea,' I said, fascinated by the constructive cogs whirring in her young mind. She broke one in half and fed it to a grateful mutt, putting the other half back into her pocket.

'That leaves just one sausage left, which I'm going to eat myself.' She nibbled a little from the top and rolled it around in her mouth to savour the flavour before finally chewing and swallowing. 'Mmm, that's very lovely,' she mused.

'I'm glad you enjoyed it,' I smiled.

'I'm afraid you can't have any,' she said. 'I've only got two; one is for Terminator and the other is for me. I would share mine with you, only I might get germs.' She had clearly thought this through.

Finally, Charmaine returned. 'Don't eat the dog's sausages, Tilly,' she snapped. Tilly quickly hid it behind her back. 'Can you believe he gave me a ticket?' she moaned, turning to me. 'I was only gone for two minutes. Two minutes, and he gave me a ticket. Sixty quid! I'm gonna need to get that back from you, Jeff. I wouldn't want it to taint our friendship so early on.' I nodded, a little baffled by her logic. I reached for that evening's pay packet. 'Are you ready to go?' I shook my head, gesturing that I had been unwilling to strip in front of Tilly. 'Well, now I'm not really sure I've still got time to wait and then drive you home. I'll call you. Come on, Tilly!' She reached out a hand to Tilly, who grasped it and followed her back out into the hall. Terminator seemed desperate to stay. I realised he was trying to get back to the sausage Tilly had guiltily dropped on the floor behind her.

As the door closed I sat alone, looking at the sausage and then at the lollipop still clinging half way up the curtain. So much for saving on a taxi!

PSYCHIC PUSSY

When I was first told a colleague of mine had been to see a psychic pussy, I wasn't sure how to react.

'No really, it's fascinating,' they said. 'It knew all about his varicose veins and bad back.' Anyone with descent eyesight would know that, I thought. But, always up for a new adventure, I decided to bite the bullet and pay a visit myself.

Being a fan of cats, I had always believed them to be psychic, and history tells us many of our ancestors had the same opinion. What intrigued me most was how the little thing would actually tell me what it had predicted. I pictured myself asking questions and it answering with two licks for "yes" and one lick and a meow for "no". Or would it perhaps stare into my eyes and send me a telepathic message?

I had to wait three weeks for my reading, as apparently it was a very busy pussy and quite elderly, so needed periods of rest between appointments. The night my consultation finally arrived, it was appropriately spooky with heavy rain, thunder and lightning. I have to confess I was actually quite excited as I parked my car outside a north London council house and ran up the broken path to the porch. The knee-high grass in the front garden darted back and forth in the whistling wind as I waited for a response to my knock. An elderly lady in a fun-fur leopard-skin onesie let me in. I wondered for a moment if she was indeed the Psychic Pussy and that the whole experience was intended to be somehow symbolic. But my nose very quickly led my eyes to a cat-litter tray behind the front door in the hall. Assuming this to be for the feline mystic and not the old lady, I followed her through to the lounge.

'I'm Maggie, would you like a cup of tea my darling?' she asked, gesturing for me to sit. 'I'll put the kettle on while I prepare the mixture.' She seemed a very lovely lady despite her criminal dress sense, but her comment concerned me a little.

'That would be nice, thank you,' I replied, 'but what kind of tea is it? I've got to drive home.'

'Oh, I've only got PG Tips dear,' she giggled. 'The mixture's not for you, it's for Sebastian.' I was guessing Sebastian was the cat, though for the moment the mixture remained a mystery.

She toddled off in the direction of the kitchen as I sank into a large overstuffed armchair and looked around the room. It was suitably dark and moody, with several large white candles strategically balanced here and there. Random flashes of lightning through a gap in the curtains shot shards of sparkling light across the furniture. Suddenly from nowhere, a large ginger ball of fluff jumped up onto my lap, purring fiercely. He adoringly snuggled his head into my hand for strokes, I was happy to oblige.

'Oh, I see you've met Sebastian,' the lady smiled, returning to the room. She placed my tea on the coffee table and handed me a wide-brimmed bowl of something brown and sludgy. 'That's for her,' she smiled, nodding towards the cat.

'Her? I thought you said Sebastian?' I asked.

'She just wandered in the back door one day out of the blue and that was the name on her collar,' said Maggie. 'She's full of mysteries.' I looked down at her sitting in my lap. She stared up at me hypnotically and blinked a few times, strangely still. 'She's got the measure of you now, you can use the mixture.' I wasn't sure what this meant.

'So, what… do I rub it in, or…'

'No, she'll eat it,' the lady laughed. Sebastian did indeed eat a little while sitting right there on my lap. What she didn't eat, she moved around a bit with her nose before jumping down and wandering off into the hall. 'Now, give it to me and I'll tell you what Sebastian is predicting for you.' I passed the bowl into Maggie's outstretched hand and she sat, pulling her glasses down from the top of her head and staring intelligently at the mixture. I held my breath and waited with anticipation. I'd had my tealeaves read before and it was quite accurate, I could see no reason why cat food would be any different.

'I can see a pair of high heels.' She had me on the first line. 'You work in a shoe shop.' Hmm. Accurate or not, this experience was going to be worth the twenty quid for entertainment value alone. 'And you like to write, I can see a pen and paper.' So far, so good. 'There are a lot of changes coming into your life very soon and it's all set to music. Is there a radiogram in your shop?' I'd figured by then that the cat was probably better at this than she was. 'And you're going to get some money you didn't know was coming very soon.' It sounded lovely.

'How did you first find out Sebastian could do this?' I asked.

'I've always done tealeaves, and I recognised the same signs in his food. He was trying to tell me something.'

'Maggie and moggy…you make a good team. Can you do my tealeaves too?' I asked hopefully.

'No sorry, that's not going to be possible.' I was a little disappointed.

'Oh, would that disrupt Sebastian's psychic balance, do you think?' I didn't want to upset the cat.

'No it's not that, my darling,' she smiled. 'I can't do your tealeaves cause I made it with a teabag.' Ask a silly question.

A few days later, I did come into a little unexpected cash. Perhaps the gorgeous Sebastian was psychic after all.

www.ingramcontent.com/pod-product-compliance
Lightning Source LLC
Chambersburg PA
CBHW030432010526
44118CB00011B/601